WHY A TRANSCENDENTAL ANTHROPOLOGY?

Why a Transcendental Anthropology?

Leonardo Polo

Translated by
Greg Chafuen
Roderrick Esclanda
Alberto I. Vargas

Leonardo Polo Institute of Philosophy Press
2015

First Edition: 2014
Second Edition: 2015

ISBN 978-0-9912568-1-5

Cover image:
Yves Klein, *Untitled Anthropometry*, (ANT 8), 1960 ca.
Dry pigment and synthetic resin on burnt paper, 102 x 73 cm
© Yves Klein, ADAGP, Paris 2014

Leonardo Polo Institute of Philosophy
1121 North Notre Dame Ave.
South Bend, IN 46617

www.leonardopoloinstitute.org

Table of Contents

Acknowledgements

Translations of this sort are the work not only of the translators, but also of many people cooperating together in a project. For this reason, the translators would first like to thank *Ediciones Rialp S.A.* for granting permission to publish the translation of this key work from Leonardo Polo. We also owe a special debt of gratitude to Daniel Moquay and the *Yves Klein Archive* for the great honor of allowing us to use a painting of the renowned painter Yves Klein for the cover of this book. Special thanks also to Paul Dumol, Marga Vega, Mark Mannion, and David González Ginocchio for suggesting corrections to the translation, and to Idoya Zorroza for the book layout. Finally, we would like to thank the *Leonardo Polo Institute of Philosophy* for publishing this first English translation of Leonardo Polo's work, and for their work at promoting the translation of his complete works. Through this work of translation, we hope that Polo's works will be warmly received by the international academic community, and will prove to be a helpful contribution to solving the many challenges posed by modern thought.

Introduction

The question, "Why a transcendental anthropology?" entails already having in some way attained the answer to the question, and yet it also calls for a justification not only of the answer, but of the question itself. In this article, the Spanish philosopher Leonardo Polo (1926-2013) presents his proposal of a transcendental anthropology and seeks to provide historical and philosophical reasons that make such a proposal timely and fitting for the present historical situation of philosophy.

In Polo's view, classical philosophy reaches its peak with a metaphysics that studies the act of being of the physical universe and with the doctrine of the metaphysical transcendental. The irreducible intimacy or personal act of being of the human person is, however, not studied in any developed way by classical philosophy.

Modern philosophy on the other hand is a philosophy of the subject. It seeks to establish the self as a radical or transcendent principle, but falls prey, according to Polo's reading, to errors that stem from the lack of a correct philosophical method. The result is a failed attempt at a transcendental anthropology.

Polo thus sees the present historical situation as one in which the discoveries of classical philosophy have to be expanded to include more properly anthropological themes and in which modern philosophy's failed attempt at a transcendental anthropology must be addressed and corrected.

Polo's own proposal makes use of the philosophical method of the abandonment of the mental limit, a method for doing philosophy that he describes as consisting in *detecting the mental limit* and in *detecting it in conditions such that it can be abandoned*. The result is a transcendental anthropology that expands the classical doctrine of the transcendentals to include anthropological transcendentals and one that is capable of critically engaging modern and contemporary philosophy, thus correcting its errors and incorporating its deepest insights into itself.

Throughout this article, Polo takes up central questions of the history of philosophy that are not yet resolved and insists on concentrating his philosophical attention on them until he arrives at a new proposal. To do this, he draws from the fruit of years of previous work and makes use of the philosophical methodology that he discovered and developed decades earlier. To help the reader obtain a better view of Leonardo Polo's philosophical project and to put the present work in perspective, this introduction is divided into two sections. The first aims to introduce Polo's methodology of the abandonment of the mental limit and his development of a transcendental anthropology by presenting it within the context of his intellectual trajectory. The second deals more directly with the context and content of "Why a Transcendental Anthropology?"

Transcendental Anthropology within Leonardo Polo's Intellectual Trajectory

First Insight Regarding the Mental Limit (1950)

Leonardo Polo's initial discovery of the methodology that he would later call the abandonment of the mental limit dates back to the spring of 1950, when he was doing research in Rome. The detection of the limit was a clear insight that came to him all of a sudden. As he recalls: "… it suddenly occurred to me, period. I was thinking about thinking and being, and about what being had to do with thinking; then I realized that we cannot arrive at being if one does not abandon the supposition of the object, because the supposition makes the object limited and a limited knowledge cannot be a knowledge of being if this is taken in the transcendental sense."

In other words, to become aware of the mental limit and of the need to abandon it is to notice that "one cannot separate, I repeat, being from being, it is not possible to take hold of it objectively because in this way it is 'des-realized'; but if being is not real, it is nothing. The intentional consideration of being is a *quid pro quo*. Being agrees with itself, but, being known *intentionaliter* is, as the Scholastics would say, an extrinsic denomination. When I know the idea, I do not in any way affect what I know, because the idea of what I know is in my mind as intelligible in act and in reality as intelligible in potency. The real distinction between essence and being makes the question all the more serious, because if being and essence were the same, then knowing something of the essence would be knowing something of being." (J. Cruz, "Filosofar hoy. Entrevista con Leonardo Polo", *Anuario Filosófico*, Vol. XXI, 1 (1992), 46-47)

This discovery would be the initial insight that Leonardo Polo would later develop into a methodology for doing philosophy, a methodology that he would later call the abandonment of the mental limit.

Early Formulation of the Abandonment of the Mental Limit in The Access to Being *(1964)*

In his early work, *The Access to Being* (1964), Leonardo Polo presents the notion of the mental limit (of objective thought) and develops it in dialogue and in contrast with Spinoza, Kant, Hegel, and Heidegger. He then puts forward his own philosophical proposal: that the mental limit can not only be detected, but that it can also be abandoned. Thus, Polo seeks not only to *discover the limits of objective thought*, but also to *detect this limit in conditions such that it is possible to abandon this limit*. This methodology, which Polo now calls the abandonment of the mental limit, has four dimensions that lead to the study of four different, but interrelated, thematic fields: (1) the study of extra-mental existence; (2) the study of the extra-mental predicamental causes (extra-mental essence); (3) the study of human existence; and (4) the study of human essence as *availing-of*.

Starting with *The Access to Being*, Polo planned a series of works that would cover these thematic fields. The first of these was to be *Being I* (on extra-mental being), followed by *Being II* (on the extra-mental essence of the universe), *Being III* (on the personal act of being), and *Being IV* (on human essence). Of these, only *Being I* was published. The subject matter of *Being II* would eventually find its way into his *Course on the Theory of Knowledge* (especially Volume IV), and those of *Being III* and *IV* would later appear as *Transcendental Anthropology I* and *II*.

Being I (1966) develops the first dimension of the abandonment of the mental limit, which focuses on extra-mental existence, that is, on the being of the physical universe. Here Polo develops a metaphysics based on a knowledge of first principles: created being as the principle of non-contradiction and as the principle of causality; and both of these distinct from, yet compatible with, the principle of identity, which is God the Creator. The study of these three principles as distinct, yet compatible first principles constitutes the central axioms of Polo's metaphysics.

The somewhat abrupt nature of the presentation of the topics in his first books, as well as their novelty, baffled a public accustomed to a more scholastic style and to a more "conventional" subject matter. Few accepted his new method for approaching important philosophical questions, and misunderstandings led many to brand him as a Hegelian or as not sufficiently "orthodox". Only a few sensed something of interest in Polo's philosophy. The poor reception among philosophers of those years may be one of the reasons that explain why Leonardo Polo did not publish the other works that he had already planned (*Being II*, *Being III* and *Being IV*) in which he was to develop his philosophy of nature and transcendental anthropology.

Polo did not, however, abandon his philosophical project, but continued his efforts to draw out the consequences and implications of his philosophical methodology. Years later, in an interview, Polo would recall, "… to detect the limit and abandon it can be done or not. If it cannot be done, it seems to me that it would be difficult to remain a realist, not in the sense of coinciding intentionally with the truth, but rather of gaining access to extra-mental being, which does not form part of what is thought. This is how I saw it, and not as a matter of originality, but rather as having found something that had to be developed, and this was a very large undertaking, and since I had thought about it in Rome, I realized that it was a work for an entire lifetime. Am I going to dedicate my life to this? If I do, I run a risk; at that time I was not capable of gauging all the implications of what this meant." (Polo, *Conversaciones, pro manuscripto*).

At another moment, he would comment: "one danger was that I would not succeed, or, if I were successful, that I would not be accepted by the community of philosophers, which meant I would be left unpublished; or, worse, publish and have no one understand (this second possibility has been almost entirely fulfilled). The second danger was to be mistaken, that is, to address an issue in such a way that I would have to backtrack later. Not so much that I would be left more or less shunned as an author, but that I would have to recant or gather together what already existed and burn it. This danger was especially serious when considering freedom as a transcendental, because it is clear that the idea of a transcendental linked with freedom appears in many modern thinkers. Thus, I could fall into those errors or be misinterpreted. A third danger was to be misunderstood; not that I would be mistaken, but that I would be the occasion for others being mistaken. Fortunately, this danger has not really materialized" (Polo, *La libertad, pro manuscripto*).

Reformulation in the Course on the Theory of Knowledge *(1984-1996)*

During the 1970s and early 80s, Polo published very little, but continued developing his ideas and finding clearer ways to present them, especially through courses on the theory of knowledge. In these courses, Polo made a special effort to describe his thought in continuity with classical philosophy, especially Aristotle, and in contrast with modern theories of knowledge, especially Spinoza, Kant, Hegel, and Heidegger. With the help of transcriptions of lecture notes taken by his students, Polo eventually put together sufficient material for the publication and a new presentation of his philosophical method. The result was the publication of his four volume *Course on the Theory of Knowledge* [Volume I (1984); Volume II (1985); Volume III (1988); Volume IV/1 (1994); and Volume IV/2 (1996)] that inaugurated a new period of publications for Polo.

In the *Course on the Theory of Knowledge*, Leonardo Polo expounds upon and redevelops his philosophical methodology (the abandonment of the mental limit) by relating and contrasting it with Aristotelian gnoseology and modern versions of the theory of knowledge, especially rationalist and idealist ones.

The work is structured in roughly the following way:

Volume I: The axioms of human knowledge and the study of sensible knowledge;

Volume II: Exposition of intellectual knowledge and its limitation;

Volume III: Study of negation (or generalization) as an operation of the intellect through the history of philosophy;

Volume IV/1 and *IV/2*: Examination of human rational operations (concept, judgment, and reasoning) and their reach from the perspective of the mental limit.

Polo continued to teach courses throughout this time, and much of the material included in the *Course on the Theory of Knowledge* drew from the maturing of his thought, especially with regard to his study of the predicamental causes and of the philosophy of nature. In this regard, the fourth volume of the *Course on the Theory of Knowledge* constitutes, in fact, the exposition of the second dimension of the mental limit (corresponding to the subject matter originally planned for *Being II*), which is directed to the extra-mental essence (also described as the quadruple con-causality of the predicamental causes) of the physical universe.

The publication of the *Course on the Theory of Knowledge* marked a maturation of Polo's presentation of his philosophical method and of the consequences of this method. In it, Polo presents a clearer exposition of intellectual operations and their limit. He also develops a philosophy of intellectual habits that make possible higher operations and allow for the partial or complete abandonment of the mental limit. Throughout the exposition, Polo develops notions such as habits and the real distinction between act of being and essence that continue classical philosophy, but also go beyond it. At the same time he engages Modern philosophers and seeks to correct their insights.

Transcendental Anthropology *(1999-2003)*

Starting in the late 1980s and continuing into the 1990s, Polo began concentrating on developing his transcendental anthropology, and the greater part of his doctoral courses were dedicated to this theme. In these years, Polo gave several doctoral courses on transcendental anthropology as well as courses on the transcendentals, freedom, the practical reason, the will and its acts, the *logos*, the self, the sentiments, and the human essence.

In these courses, Polo continued with his practice of lecturing and then of taking the transcriptions of notes made by his students to further develop and clarify his thought while preparing eventual publications. One of these courses would later become the basis of "Why a Transcendental Anthropology" which is the last chapter of *The Present and Future of Man* (1993), a work that includes other earlier studies that focus on the anthropological consequences of his methodology of the abandonment of the mental limit.

After his retirement in 1996, Polo continued working on his philosophical anthropology and finally published *Transcendental Anthropology I* in 1999 and *Transcendental Anthropology II* in 2003. These two works cover the subject matter that Polo had originally intended for *Being III* and *Being IV* in the 1960s, and thus bring Polo's philosophical project to completion. In the prologue of the first volume, Polo refers to his work on transcendental anthropology as the culmination of his philosophical work in which all his other works can finally be seen from their proper perspective: "This book is certainly the culmination of my philosophical inquiry. What I mean by this is that the method that has led up to it no longer gives more of itself. But, since this method makes possible access to abundant thematic fruits, this book is added to the harvest that is contained, but not exhausted in other writings. Because of its double value (methodological and thematic), the summit reopens the various thematic areas: it reiterates them" (*Transcendental Anthropology I*, Prologue).

Transcendental Anthropology I contains the first part of the transcendental anthropology that Polo proposes as fruit of the third dimension of the abandonment of the mental limit. In it Polo justifies the need for an anthropology that is transcendental by distinguishing between the act of being of the physical universe (studied in metaphysics) and the act of being of the human person (the subject matter of transcendental anthropology). With this, Polo seeks to study the being of the human person on the level of act of being, but at the same time to distinguish this transcendental anthropology from metaphysics. A consequence of this is his proposal to expand the medieval theory of transcendentals to include transcendentals that are anthropological in nature. From this perspective, the being of the human person is studied on a transcendental level as *co-existence*, *transcendental freedom*, *personal intellection*, and *gift-love*. These personal transcendentals form the nucleus of Leonardo Polo's proposal for a transcendental anthropology.

Transcendental Anthropology II contains the second part of the transcendental anthropology that Polo proposes as fruit of the fourth and final dimension of the abandonment of the mental limit. From this perspective, Polo studies the manifestation of the person, which is human essence or, rather, the self: her body and her higher faculties (the intelligence and the will) as well as their acts and acquired habits. With the publication of this second volume of *Transcendental Anthropology*, it can be said that the major elements of Polo's philosophy had finally been made public.

Introduction to "Why a Transcendental Anthropology?"

The article "Why a Transcendental Anthropology?" first appeared in Spanish as the final chapter of *The Present and Future of Man* (1993). This work was edited by Ricardo Yepes and published in 1993 as a way of introducing Polo's transcendental anthropology to a wider public. It is composed of seven articles written by Polo, some previously published, others not, but all re-elaborated for publication in this work.

The goal of *The Present and Future of Man* is to show how Polo's proposal draws from the classical tradition of philosophy, especially from Aristotle's notion of act and immanent operation and Thomas Aquinas's real distinction between essence and act of being. At the same time, it aims to situate Polo's transcendental anthropology in its context of critical dialogue with modern philosophy (especially Hegel) and with its concerns regarding subjectivity as well as the situation of crisis in philosophy in the contemporary world.

The first six chapters of the book seek to show this continuity and to describe how the present vision of the human person arose historically. These chapters cover topics related to the continuing philosophical relevance of Aristotle, the knowledge of God and the crisis of medieval philosophy, the modern view of human operative action, the state of philosophy in our current situation, knowledge as a vital activity, and the awareness of crisis in contemporary culture.

The seventh article, "Why a Transcendental Anthropology?" (the subject of this present translation) is based on the first five lectures of a twelve lecture long course on transcendental anthropology that Polo gave at the Universidad Panamericana (Mexico) in the summer of 1987. In these lectures, Polo directly introduces the theme of transcendental anthropology: he explains what this proposal consists of, why it is fitting at this moment of the history of philosophy, the methodology that is required for investigating it properly, and a brief sketch of the themes that it involves.

In "Why a Transcendental Anthropology?," Polo points out the limitations of metaphysics and how it cannot adequately present the theme of radical human freedom. Metaphysics arrives at an act of being as ground by discovering what is primary in the extra-mental physical universe. From this perspective, however, freedom can be studied only within the categorical order (as a property of human acts, and, more particularly, of voluntary acts), but not in its radicality as primary or transcendental. For Polo, personal being is just as or even more real than the act of being of the universe, but is neither ground nor grounded. Thus, there is a need to rethink the notion of the transcendental and to expand it so as to properly attain the transcendental character of personal being. The result is an expansion of the transcendentals to what Polo calls the personal or anthropological transcendentals. In this article, Polo mentions co-being, transcendental freedom and being *additionally*. In other works, Polo includes other personal transcendentals, namely, *personal intellection* and *gift-being*. This is the transcendental anthropology that Polo proposes.

At various moments in the article, Polo makes reference to modern philosophy and its interest in the subject and in freedom. In his reading of the history of philosophy, Polo points out that modern philosophy aspired to a transcendental philosophy of the self, but failed to do so correctly and oftentimes mistakenly attempted to substitute metaphysics with a transcendental philosophy focused on freedom. In Polo's analysis, the failure of modern philosophy is due to the lack of a correct philosophical method or to the use of an inadequate one. The solution, according to Polo, lies in discovering the adequate method for investigating the philosophical theme of transcendental freedom.

The correct methodology for a transcendental anthropology would, according to Polo, be one that is capable of treating freedom as transcendental, while at the same time distinguishing it from the metaphysical themes. Here, Polo makes use of the philosophical method of the *abandonment of the mental limit*, which is central to the development of his philosophy since the 1950s. Hence, it would not be incorrect to say that Polo's proposal of a transcendental anthropology is, in fact, a consequence of this philosophical method.

Polo's discussion of the abandonment of the mental limit is the most difficult part of this article, and a much more extensive presentation of the methodology can be found in his four volume *Course on the Theory of Knowledge* and in the first volume of his *Transcendental Anthropology*. Although a complete presentation of Polo's theory of knowledge is not possible here, it may be helpful to point out some of its general lines.

The initial act of human intellectual knowing is operative knowing. Following Aristotle, Polo maintains that knowing is an immanent act, that is, an act in which the act or operation is commensurate and simultaneous with its object. Thus, just as I see what I see while I see, I think what is thought (the object of thought) while I think. In this view, operation and object are commensurate and simultaneous and therefore while there is an operation, there is an object. Consequently, there is never an operation of knowing without an object and there is never an object without a corresponding act or operation of knowing.

Another characteristic of operative knowing is the unicity of the object thought. It is this unicity that forms the limit of operational knowing. Thus, going beyond the knowledge of the object requires detecting this unicity or limit. This cannot, however, be done by the operation itself nor by any other operation since operations only know objects, but do not know acts or operations. Thus, what is needed is a higher cognitive act, but one that is not an operation. Polo calls these acts habits, and it is by intellectual habits that the unicity or limit of operations and the operations themselves are known.

Polo's abandonment of the mental limit consists precisely in this: to detect the mental limit in conditions such that it can be abandoned. In the present article, Polo points out that the mental limit can be abandoned in four ways. By abandoning the mental limit trans-objectively, that is, by going beyond the intentional object, one arrives at knowledge of the extra-mental act of being of the physical universe (the theme of metaphysics) and at knowledge of the quadruple con-causality of predicamental causes (the theme of philosophy of nature). The mental limit can, however, also be abandoned along the line of the operation, that is, trans-operatively or trans-immanently. And in this way one arrives at what Polo calls the intimacy or being of the human person (the theme of transcendental anthropology) and at the human essence as *availing-of* (the theme of the anthropology of the human essence).

With his theory of knowledge Polo clearly distinguishes the various philosophical themes and makes possible the correct study of these themes without confusing them with each other. He is thereby able to re-elaborate themes from classical philosophy, especially Thomas Aquinas's real distinction between act of being and essence. At the same time, he is able to address the concerns of modern philosophy without falling into the errors and confusion that befell it and thus is able to correct them. But, most importantly, it makes possible the expansion of the real distinction to anthropology, thus giving rise to the study of the personal or anthropological transcendentals that form the theme of transcendental anthropology. In this article, Polo focuses on three of these anthropological transcendentals: *co-existence*, *transcendental freedom*, and being *additionally*.

Polo describes the personal act of being that is compatible yet distinct from the act of being of the universe as *co-existence*. Thus, the person is not limited to being: she is co-being, co-existing, being-with. One dimension of this co-existing is co-existence with the act of being of the physical universe. The person co-exists with being as ground, but cannot be reduced to it. It is thus clear that the theme of transcendental anthropology is distinct from that of metaphysics, yet compatible with it.

Insofar as the abandonment of the mental limit leads to a knowledge of freedom that is not simply limited to the freedom of voluntary acts or to freedom of choice, but rather as convertible with personal co-being, then the personal act of being can also be called *transcendental freedom.* Polo points out that the metaphysical sense of being does not lead to freedom; instead, freedom is found only in anthropology and as a reality that neither grounds nor is grounded. At the same time, however, transcendental freedom is compatible with and co-exists with extra-mental reality.

Human personal being can also be described as being *additionally.* Insofar as the personal act of being or co-existing is known as irreducible intimacy, it co-is *additionally.*

The personal act of being is, in the first place, *additionally* to the object of thought and to operative knowing. Thus, the person can never be adequately captured by objective thought, nor is the personal act of being to be confused with the operation of knowing. It is, so to say, always *additionally* to thought: it is inexhaustible and overflowing light, the pure non-exhausting itself when operatively knowing.

A consequence of this is that knowledge of the human person is attained only insofar as *additionally.* That is, the correct knowledge of the personal act of being is attained only as knowledge of an act that is being (or better, co-being) *additionally,* never as something finished or as a result. This means that the personal act of being can only be known by a methodology that *accompanies* its being *additionally.* Thus, being *additionally* can also be described as *future without defuturization* and, once again, as *transcendental freedom.*

The adverb *additionally* (*además* in Spanish) also clearly distinguishes the personal act of being from the act of being of the universe. Polo characterizes the extra-mental act of being of the universe as *beginning that neither ceases nor is followed* and as *persistence.* The personal act of being on the other hand is characterized as being *additionally.* *Additionally* thus makes reference to the distinction between the extra-mental act of being of the universe and the co-existing act of being of the human person on a transcendental level, as what marks the distinction of one from another *qua* act of being. With this, the transcendental character of the anthropology that Polo proposes is clear.

Throughout "Why a Transcendental Anthropology?," Polo's use of the abandonment of the mental limit makes possible a transcendental anthropology that continues the great philosophical discoveries of classical metaphysics, corrects modern philosophy on its own terms, and responds to the needs of the current historical situation. However, although important themes are presented in this article, it must be kept in mind that it is just an introductory exploration of the theme, and as such does not present a complete vision of Polo's proposal of a transcendental anthropology. For this reason, "Why a Transcendental Anthropology?" is merely a beginning that seeks to justify the undertaking of a transcendental anthropology, and offers an initial approach that opens up a path that can lead to the development of a more complete transcendental anthropology. Much of the material presented here is later taken up, continued, re-elaborated, and combined with other material to produce two important works that complete Polo's philosophical anthropology: *Transcendental Anthropology I* (1999) and *Transcendental Anthropology II* (2003). For now, we present this introductory article translated into English for the first time so that we might, with Polo, ask, "Why a Transcendental Anthropology?"

Greg Chafuen, Roderrick Esclanda, and Alberto I. Vargas
South Bend, Indiana, February 5, 2014

Why a Transcendental Anthropology?[*]

Leonardo Polo

The notion of immanent operation appears repeatedly throughout *Curso de teoría del conocimento* [*Course on the Theory of Knowledge*]. It is one of the central issues that I strive to present. Knowledge is an act. One knows only in act. This is the Aristotelian approach that I propose to axiomatically formulate. In any case, among cognitive acts, the immanent operation is, shall we say, the lowest. One can operatively know, exercising operations. This is how the sensibility and the intelligence know (human intellectual knowledge is also operative). But one can intellectually know [*inteligir*] in a way that is above operations, or in a non-operative mode, since, as I insist, the cognitive operation is not the supreme or superior cognitive act. Also, no operation knows itself (rather, it knows the object that it possesses), and thus it is not even possible to know that one knows with operations if a superior act does not manifest them.

In that *Course on the Theory of Knowledge*, I also propose with regard to this what I call the *axiom of hierarchy*: when it is a question of knowledge (or as long as we are dealing with the created immaterial), the most appropriate or most correct distinction is the distinction of grade, hierarchy, and not simple numerical distinction. It involves distinctions between the

---

    *   Originally published in POLO, L. (1993), *Presente y futuro del hombre*, Rialp, Madrid, pp. 149-203. This translation is based on the corrected 2012 edition (pp. 142-194). Translated by Greg Chafuen, Roderick Esclanda and Alberto I. Vargas.

superior and the inferior. Now, I insist, operative knowledge is inferior knowledge. Above it, other levels or modes of knowing exist—other types of cognitive acts, among which we can highlight three: (1) habitual knowledge (I consider this as knowledge in act, although not actual, which is superior to operative knowledge); (2) knowledge as act of being: *ipsum Esse subsistens*, that is, God; or (3) as *esse hominis*. In the case of divine knowledge, the supreme act of knowing is convertible with originating being. In the case of man it cannot be said that the act of being is originating.

Now, if one accepts this approach, I believe that we can arrive at what I proposed in other books that were published before the *Course on the Theory of Knowledge* in the 1960s: *El acceso al ser* [*The Access to Being*] and *El ser I* [*Being I*]. In those books I lay out a way, a method for addressing the major questions of metaphysics, and, along with that, the thesis that with this method one can also distinguish metaphysics from anthropology on a transcendental level. This is what I usually call the *expansion of the transcendental* [*ampliación de lo trascendental*].

There is a correct and valid metaphysical approach that is developed in the great tradition of Western philosophy, mainly by Aristotle. I believe, however—and this is not in the classics—that this approach can be expanded. Or, in other words: if one accepts assigning metaphysics (first philosophy) the task of addressing what are, already in Plato and in Aristotle, but without calling it such, transcendental themes, and which are formulated as such by the medievals; if one accepts that metaphysics is transcendental philosophy or philosophy of the transcendentals (first philosophy, which is also the proper Aristotelian designation), then anthropology is, without it being metaphysics and being distinct from it, also transcendental.

Why? The justification for what I call the expansion of the transcendental approach is rather complex—it has to do with motives and concerns regarding historical and systematic problems. But if what I propose is correct, this correction rests (supposing that the theme of metaphysics is being), above all, in that the being of man is not the being that metaphysics deals with. The being that metaphysics deals with is being as principle, or rather the principial sense of being. This sense does not include freedom. Being a principle does not mean being free. For this reason, in an approach that only detects or only achieves attaining knowledge of being as principle (or the fundamental sense of being), that is, that which is first (because first philosophy deals with what is first, and that which is first is the principle), and given that principle does not include freedom (it is not equivalent to it; freedom is not a principle), freedom is considered as a merely categorical issue. Assimilated to the categorical order, freedom is understood as a property of certain types of acts—concretely, of voluntary acts, and nothing more.

Now, as I see it, this is insufficient for freedom. Freedom must be placed on the transcendental level, but it cannot be understood from principial being. It cannot be understood as grounded*, because a grounded freedom is contradictory. The notion of freedom is not preserved in a dependent and grounded freedom—this is the nullification of the very notion of freedom. In order to be free it is important, not so much to be independent, but rather to not be preceded by a deeper or more radical instance and, therefore, not to be grounded. However, neither must freedom be confused with the ground. It does not belong to freedom either to be grounded or to be ground. Neither of these two things is compatible with freedom. This is one of the concerns and one of the motives that lead to this expansion: to open up or make space for a specific transcendental value for freedom.

It is evident that this cannot be done if we consider only the metaphysical because the metaphysical (as its name indicates, and in this regard Andronicus of Rhodes's designation is a good one) is what is *beyond the physical*. It is transcendental as *trans-physical*—it is what is primary with respect to the physical. But what is primary with respect to the physical does not lead to freedom.

---

* The Spanish word *fundamento* can also be translated as foundation or fundament (note of the translators).

Where freedom is discovered, or where freedom appears, is, precisely, in anthropology—it is not a discovery of what is extra-mental, beyond, etc. This (the extra-mental) is validly transcendental—it is a correct sense of the transcendental. But human being is just as real as, or even more real than, the universe. Thus, there must be a sense of the transcendental that is not metaphysical, but rather is precisely anthropological.

But, how? What new realm of the transcendental is thereby drawn? If one speaks of the *trans-physical*, then one can also speak of the *trans-operative*. It is precisely the consideration of knowledge as operation, insofar as knowledge as operation is not the highest (knowledge is always act, but the operation is not the highest act of knowing), that makes it possible to affirm that one can establish a transcending with respect to operating—a transcending along the line, shall we say, of the operation.

What was just presented can also be said in this way: human knowledge is knowledge of object. For example, to think-thought with regard to intellectual operations, or to see-what-is-seen, etc. when it comes to sensible operation. When it comes to operations (in the deepest sense this refers to the intellectual ones, which are higher, since a hierarchy among the operations also exists), one can say that, if I objectively know or know in an operative way, what I know is what is known in act, is what is called the intentional. Now, if it is possible to speak of the trans-operative (and not only of the trans-physical), then there will be a knowledge that is transcendental with respect to objective knowledge, and what is known by it will be superior to what is intentionally known. If operative knowledge is not the highest, it cannot exhaust the knowable. Therefore, one cannot know the transcendental in an objective manner. It is necessary to transcend the object. This transcending the object (insofar as transcending the object that is thought) is a transcending that leads to metaphysics.

If we consider not only the known, the object, but rather the act of knowing that is the operation, then we will realize that the transcendental with respect to the operation exists. And this is precisely the transcendental along the line of the spirit. On the level of the object we do not possess the spirit. The proper object of objective knowing is the *quidditas sensibilis*, but not the spirit. With regard to the *quidditas sensibilis* as object, I can establish the transcendental as trans-objective, or beyond what I capture as object. But this refers to the known. On the other hand, if I keep in mind the knowing, I also have to say that the operation is not transcendental; but there is a sense of the transcendental that needs to be discovered along the line of the operation, or transcending the operation—not transcending the object, but rather the operation.

It can be said that transcending the object is an extra-mental transcending, which brings me beyond the object thought. It leads me to the radicality of the object of thought, since it allows me to return the object of thought to reality—for example, to the predicamental formal cause; and from the predicamental cause, I can go to the transcendental principial, since knowing the unified sense of the physical causes allows me to arrive at being as ground, or at the principial sense of being. Now, if transcending the object leads to the extra-mental, transcending the operation makes it possible to attain another sense of the transcendental that is distinct from the metaphysical or extra-mental transcendental. Because the act of knowing is not extra-mental. The act of knowing cannot be more distinct than itself: it is in no way extra-mental; it cannot be beyond. And if the operation is not the highest act of knowing, then it is evident that the operation must also be transcended. But when transcending the operation (not the object possessed by the operation, but rather the operation itself), we must find the spiritual transcendental, not the trans-physical or metaphysical, but rather, so to say, the *trans-immanent*. And there, along this line, is where one can place freedom as transcendental: transcendental freedom.

I do not know if the above mentioned distinction is clearly seen. But I believe that it must be established. It is necessary to accept the (shall we say) dual character of operative knowledge in which, on the one hand, there is the operation of knowing and, on the other, that which the

5

operation possesses, which is precisely what is known: the object. The object of knowing is not the operation of knowing; the operation of knowing cannot be known in objective terms. On the one hand, we have the object and, on the other, the act of knowing the object. They are intimately united, but cannot be confused.

Now, the consideration of the object can lead us from the physical to the trans-physical. It is in this way that I discover metaphysics. However, with this, it is not the operation of knowing that has been taken into consideration, but rather the object known by the operation. But if the operation of knowing is sufficiently discernible from the object known, then it is also possible to transcend, or go beyond, along the line of the operation. And this cannot be called trans-physical or metaphysical because the operation of knowing is not physical. "Metaphysics" is a good designation because physical reality exists, and beyond that is the metaphysical, to which I arrive at by transcending the physical, so to say. But transcending the operation insofar as it is an operation of knowing (insofar as it is an immanent operation) does not lead to the trans-physical, but rather to a transcending along the line of the spirit, because the operation as such is immaterial. That which is objectively or intentionally known is also immaterial, but it is intentional; it refers to the material, to physical realities. Its immateriality is only intentional. And it is intentional with respect to the physical. In contrast, it cannot in any way be said that the immanent operation is physical, not even that it is intentional with respect to the physical. What is intentional is the object, not the operation.

In accordance with this, the metaphysical transcendental is justified, and a transcendental metaphysics can be done. But this is not all: a duality, so to say, is opened up. What has been developed by following the great Greek and Medieval discoveries? Strictly speaking, a metaphysics and a physics. For its part, psychology is an intermediate science in which some human themes appear. Not, however, the theme of person, which does not fit in well with the focus of this science. As I see it, psychology falls short in this regard, and it seems to me necessary to develop it.

In any case, what I call *expansion of the transcendental* (a transcendental anthropology as distinct from metaphysics) is not strictly necessary. If it were, it would be necessary to say that there is a positive *lapsus* in classical philosophy, something that I do not accept. But it certainly can be said that the line of investigation that begins with the consideration of the immanent operation as an operation (not of its object, but rather of the operation itself) and which gives rise to a transcendental anthropology, is barely developed in classical philosophy in a developed form.

Is it necessary to do so? No. Is it fitting? Is it appropriate to do so? Yes. Moreover, this opportunity is precisely our situation, our historical present, and this is because one of the keys of modern philosophy is the attempt to produce a transcendental anthropology. Modern philosophy is a philosophy of the subject. If one does not venture to open up the field of transcendental anthropology, then it would have to be said that if classical philosophy is correct, and if classical metaphysics is valid, then, nevertheless, the thematic expansion that modern philosophy attempts cannot be assimilated by the classical thinker or by one who accepts classical philosophy and begins with it. There would be something like an estrangement between classical and modern philosophy. This estrangement is frequently admitted—it is said that they are two irreconcilable philosophies; and it is even said that modern philosophy is dangerous and false, that it amounts to an anthropocentrism, etc. However nothing is gained by these reluctant or allergic reactions. Thinking a transcendental anthropology is needed.

Certainly, transcendental anthropology is not necessary. It can also be argued that what the modern philosophers attempted was a mistake and that modern philosophy is refuted. Answer: yes; it contains many errors. But the spirit is still nevertheless irreducible to the physical. The spirit is not physical. The knowing subject is not the principle of the physical, or vice versa—the physical does not know. One does not arrive at the spirit along the line of the physical; or if one does arrive at it, one arrives in a very weak way. A predicamental consideration of man that leaves anthropology as a second philosophy may be enough. It might be sufficient. However, without it being absolutely necessary, to the degree possible (and our historical situation counsels it) the development of a transcendental philosophy is fitting. And here "fitting" might refer to something more than "necessary", because it points to something like a duty. We must not stop along this line—it is a duty precisely because modern philosophy has not correctly proposed a transcendental philosophy. If it had done so, we could be excused; it would have been enough to complete classical philosophy with the modern, making the corrections that would be necessary for fitting them in well, etc. But it is fitting precisely because modern philosophy has erred. Nevertheless, that modern philosophy is wrong does not mean that the attempt at finding a transcendental anthropology is a mistake, but rather that modern anthropology is not, strictly speaking, transcendental. In other words, the anthropology of modern philosophy is a mistake with regard to the transcendentality of human being. Transcendental anthropology is fitting, not only because the philosopher must strive to study as much as possible, without giving up and without falling short, but also even more so when doing so corrects modern philosophy. Modern philosophy must be corrected on its own terms, not with arguments taken from classical philosophy, because classical philosophy is metaphysics and modern anthropology is not really a metaphysics. The non-extrinsic correction of the modern attempt on its own terms, without it coming from another instance, is a transcendental anthropology, assuming that the notion of transcendental anthropology is not a delusion. But the fact that the moderns were wrong must not lead us to think that it is a delusion, because an error must never produce a paralysis. Were they wrong? Then is it the case that what they point to cannot be thought? No. Rather, let us see why and in what they were wrong.

8

The intention of modern philosophy is evident. When Kant says that he is going to bring about a Copernican revolution, he cannot be clearer: it is a question of turning traditional philosophy on its head. That is where his idea of the legislative self is. Kantian philosophy is a philosophy of the subject. Kant has errors, yes. But the intention is very clear. It is another question whether he is frustrated in his attempt, whether Kant does not know how to bring it about, or if he does so poorly. But again, mistakes are no reason for giving up. And even less so for allowing a line of thought that belongs to us to be snatched away. This is so because the theme of the person is not Greek, but rather Christian. A man who is saved, a redeemed man (for whom God has died), is a very serious theme. God did not die for ants, nor for sheep, but for man.

These indications are made, first of all, in an attempt to justify the designation "transcendental anthropology" and, moreover, to clarify what is meant by it. It is transcendental anthropology and not something else—not predicamental anthropology, nor psychology. It is a philosophy of the spirit. And if metaphysics makes discovery of the transcendental possible, then when it comes to the spirit much more will be achieved, because the being of the spirit cannot be the being of the material. Therefore, the approach of the transcendental must be expanded. Now, to speak of transcendental anthropology is an expansion of the transcendental approach, and is not a subordination of anthropology to metaphysics. If it were subordination, I insist, then anthropology would be a second philosophy according to the sense that this expression has in tradition, and for this very reason would not be transcendental.

I insist. In the final analysis modern philosophy is a major attempt at achieving a transcendental anthropology; but it is a failed attempt. That it is a failed attempt does not mean that the venture as such is unreasonable, but rather that it has been poorly undertaken. Thus, with a transcendental anthropology two things are achieved. On the one hand, an expansion of the transcendental approach, which is justified. On the other hand, combat with modern philosophy on its own terrain, and not from metaphysics. Is it fitting? Yes. Is it indispensable or absolutely necessary? No, because it would be sufficient to refute the moderns in this order of things, and, by extension of the criteria of analogy (which is what is used in metaphysics), to address the topic of man. In this way a rather correct anthropology is achieved. But it is not transcendental and, therefore, falls short; it does not fail, it is not wrong, but it develops its proper theme very little.

These considerations have to be made in order to establish what is intended. The scope of the approach is no more nor less than this: the being of man is not the being that metaphysics deals with, nor can it be. The metaphysical treatment of the being of man is analogical and nothing more. It is carried out by a certain extension or extrapolation, one that does not allow dealing with man in a transcendental sense; it only allows for making anthropology a second philosophy. Framing the philosophy of man as a second philosophy is not mistaken, but it falls short; man deserves more. The study of man is not exhausted in this way. The verdict that the being of man is not the being of the universe (which is the being that metaphysics deals with) invites us to the expansion of the transcendental. This may sound bad, because this expansion has been attempted, but not achieved, by the moderns. For this reason it is at the same time a question of making a fundamental critique of modern philosophy on its own territory. That modern philosophy is incorrect does not entail that the territory that it explores is illusionary, since what it tried to discover is worth being discovered. One should not give up.

Man as being that co-exists. The four dimensions of abandoning the mental limit.

With a minimal number of and barely developed indications, we have seen that transcendental anthropology or (what amounts to the same) the proposal for an expansion of the classical transcendental approach can have a correct meaning and not lack justification. I am now going to attempt to present how I have addressed this task, and how I have opened up a path towards it. I understood this many years ago—there was no other way (without it being strictly necessary) but to philosophically deal with a sense of being that, although it is not reduced to the being of metaphysics, does not exclude it and is completely compatible with it. Responding to this conviction is a conference of mine called *The co-existence of man.*

To begin with, if one accepts that being and existing are equivalent, then transcendental anthropology is the doctrine regarding the being of man as co-existence. Man is not limited to being; rather, human being is co-existence (co-being or being-with). The being that corresponds to metaphysics is existing. If anthropology is not reduced to metaphysics, this is because the being of man is more than existing and being: it is co-being, co-existing; it is being-with: among others, with the being of metaphysics. The history of metaphysics is the development of the consideration of being in the principial sense. But now, if it is fitting to add the theme of man as irreducible to metaphysics, it will be necessary to insert him as being-with. Or, as Heidegger says, although without developing it, the being of man is *mit-sein* (co-being, co-existence). More than saying that man is, one should say that he "co-is": he co-exists.

The being of man is second being (not in the sense of second or derived philosophies) in the sense that he cannot be solitary. The being of man cannot be the only being, or the sense of being as solitary being. Therefore, coherently, the existing of man has to be *co-existing.* In terms of co-existence, human being is compatible with principial being (which is not second), and at the same time the transcendental expansion rests within it. The notion of co-existence contains within it the connotations of compatibility and of expansion; with this notion taken in the transcendental, ultimate, or radical sense, both are justified.

Co-existing cannot be reduced to that with which it co-exists; it is an expansion of the existing. It is not reduced to it because the being of the universe does not co-exist with the being of man. The transcendental that metaphysics deals with is not an existence or co-existent: it simply exists; it is and nothing more. In contrast, the being of man is not only being: it is co-being, *mit-sein*. Why is the being of man not reduced to the being of the universe? Because man co-exists and the universe does not.

The being of the universe does not refer to co-existence. With this, we at least propose a name for this being that is not reduced to the being of the universe. Co-existence designates the being of man as a being that is not reduced to existing. It can be said that the universe exists, but not that it co-exists. It can be said that man exists, but this is not enough; it should be said that he co-exists. The expansion is obvious, but it is an expansion that, so to speak, redounds upon what it expands. It is not simply a question of dilating, of adding, or of putting one thing next to another, that is, on the one hand metaphysics (the universe) and on the other anthropology (man). Not that. The expansion is proper to what it expands. When man exists, it is precisely co-existing that he adds to existing, but understood properly: he adds to it insofar as he gathers it to himself, because this expansion is proper of man in strict compatibility with the universe.

For this reason, transcendental anthropology is an expansion and not an elimination of metaphysics (as it was for Kant), no matter how much it is not reduced to it. The Kantian doctrine of the subject leads to metaphysical agnosticism. Nevertheless, opening a path toward transcendental anthropology does not require falling into metaphysical agnosticism, but rather quite the opposite. Co-existing shows that there is expansion and compatibility at the same time. It points to the fact that the being of man is not reducible to the being of the universe, but at the same time that it is an expansion that is respectful of it, because being is co-existent with the universe.

It might be objected that this indication of human being as co-existing is merely linguistic. It is not so. The development that allows for this notion will make known the content of transcendental anthropology.

In any case, if the being of man is not considered as co-existence, then there is no justification for speaking of transcendental anthropology as an expansion of the transcendental. Because the being of man is the being that is not limited to being, but rather has co-existing as intrinsic to it. Only insofar as he co-exists? This "only" really is merely indicative. Because co-existing points to richness, not solitariness. "Only" is a reductive notion. Perhaps there is no other choice but to use it. But the transcendental consideration of human being (as irreducible to the universe) excludes monism. In contrast, metaphysics does not exclude monism as clearly. The proof of this is that the first Greek metaphysicians (concretely, Parmenides) were monists, and monism (one solitary being) frequently surrounds metaphysics.

Now, man is not a solitary being. He is not an only (*mónon*) being, but rather *co-being*. Co-existence is not inferior to the *mónon*, but rather the opposite. It is the orientation toward the transcendental expansion. Without it, transcendental anthropology cannot be done without erring. The error of modern anthropology is that in it the expansion is attempted and frustrated—starting with the interest for the being of man, it falls into monism, and this is incompatible with man. The transcendental expansion does not mean *mónon*.

The possibility of falling into monism accompanies philosophy, frequently inserts itself into it, and even dominates it. Plotinus, for example speaks of man as *mónon*: man is the only one [*el único*] in search of fusion with the only one (*mónon pròs mónou*). But this is a bad approach. The prestige of the one is what transcendental anthropology must eliminate. The condition of possibility (to say it methodologically) of transcendental philosophy is the exclusion of monism. Because if we say that the being of man is reduced to the being of metaphysics (or that of metaphysics to that of man), then metaphysics (or anthropology) acquires an almost inevitable monistic character. For example, with regard to man, it eliminates that he co-exists. On the other hand, if we do not reduce the being of man to metaphysical being, and if we maintain the co-existence of man, what is gained is not strictly necessary or indispensable, but it certainly is very fitting—it is an extraordinarily important indication: that being does not signify *mónon*. If being signifies *mónon*, then transcendental anthropology is nullified. Therefore, the height of the error is not monism, but rather that monism appears when attempting the transcendental expansion.

If one considers nothing more than the transcendental with respect to the physical, then one can arrive at the notion of the one as solitary—the universe and nothing else. *Tò pân*, pantheism, it is usually called. The being of Parmenides, or what the Stoics say: the universe is "one". In the final analysis there exists nothing but the "one". Thus, it decays inasmuch as there is a plurality or duality. The dyad, says Plato in the *Philebus*, is imperfection; the perfect is the *mónon*. Or, more generally, this is seen in the Greek approach of the one and the many. We can accept it metaphysically, although it is also incorrect; but if it regards the being of man, then monism is pure incoherence—the gravest *quid pro quo* that one can fall into.

For this reason, modern anthropology is a mistake, a frustration of the expansion of the transcendental. The Copernican turn is a transposition of the *mónon*. With this nothing is gained. If there is some gain, it is because one realizes that *mónon* is inferior to co-existing.

14

It is therefore clear that in order to be able to justifiably attempt a transcendental anthropology (an expansion of the transcendental), it is necessary to change direction; that is, it would be good to eliminate the prestige of the one. When expanding the transcendental we cannot fall into monism (that would be the height of ineptitude), because that would be tantamount to attempting to make our way to man by making that which he leaves behind appear in him: that supposed transcendental character that the being of man excludes. It would be a case of having the opposite intended effect—an incoherence, a total failure. That is the case with Spinoza, Kant, Hegel … Transposing monism to man is an error raised to the second power. If it is already a mistake in metaphysics, then in anthropology it is a disaster.

Thus, contrary to what Plato thought, the dyad has transcendental value, and as such is a gain: it is superior to the *mónon*. Monism is a drag on metaphysics that needs to be controlled in anthropology. Only in this way can one begin a transcendental anthropology. Co-existence implies duality. If one accepts the prestige of being "only one" from monism, then duality is imperfection. And it has to be derived from the *mónon*. For Plotinus, plurality is likened to the decompression, or dissipation, of the one.

Now, in order to undertake a transcendental anthropology a larger perspective is necessary—co-existing is more perfect, shall we say, than existing; the being of man is superior to the being that metaphysics deals with, to the being of the universe. Accordingly, anthropology is also superior to metaphysics on the transcendental level, but understood well, without this implying rivalry or opposition. This does not imply having to choose between the two. Precisely if the being of man appears as co-existence, there is no incompatibility between man and the world, between anthropology and metaphysics. It is not a question of choosing: *aut, aut*. In no way would this be setting the *mónon* up as criteria. If the being of man is co-existence, there is no *aut*. That is, it is not a question of a dialectic or negative distinction. The being of man is not the negation of the being of the universe; it is, rather, its confirmation. Anthropology, instead, confirms metaphysics; it does not oppose nor substitute metaphysics. In order to understand this it is necessary to eliminate the monist criterion, the prestige of the "one", because if the *mónon* is the highest, then co-existence cannot be an expansion in the transcendental sense. They are two approaches, and it is precisely the prestige of the monist focus that ruined modern anthropology. Openness toward the theme of the subject—modern subjectivism—is a mistake with regard to anthropology insofar as it drags one to monism, to solipsism; and in this same way this theme (the subject) is approached poorly. Because the subject has to co-exist; if not, it cannot be. The notion of a solitary subject is absurd. How is this known? By anthropology, because the notion of subject is anthropological[1].

If transcendental anthropology is to be not merely the declaration of a theme, but also a method and a way to develop the expansion of the transcendental, then the key to developing this approach lies in the consideration, from a certain perspective, of unicity. It is precisely this unicity (that is how I describe it in the second volume of my *Course on the Theory of Knowledge*) that is the mental presence. And what is the mental presence? It is the consideration of the mental operation. And this (as also mentioned in the aforementioned work) is the *mental limit*. Thus, the method by which one may speak of metaphysics and of anthropology without their mutual substitution or incompatibility is *the abandonment of the mental limit*. It is precisely the abandonment of the mental limit that is the method by which the being of man can be studied without it being incompatible with the being of the universe.

---

1 The notion of subject is either anthropological or it has an anthropological sense that is not metaphysical. Subject in the metaphysical sense means substance or *hypokeimenon*. From this, one then arrives at one single substance (Spinoza). But subject in the anthropological sense does not mean substance, but rather I or person. Any confusion in this regard ruins the transcendental anthropology approach—it introduces metaphysical traits into anthropology, and thus there is no longer any such transcendental expansion.

The abandonment of the mental limit—detecting it and abandoning it—is dealt with in *El acceso al ser* [*Access to Being*], a book that I published in 1964. There I made an overall presentation of this approach in the following way: the abandonment of the mental limit opens up four major themes inasmuch as this abandonment can be done in four ways—it is methodologically quadruple. The areas that are made accessible, or those to which access is gained to the extent that the mental limit is abandoned, are: on the one hand, that which I normally call extra-mental being, that is, the being that metaphysics deals with, and extra-mental essence. On the other hand, there are two other thematic areas: human co-existence and the human essence. For this reason, after explaining what the abandonment of the mental limit means, or rather after presenting and establishing the methodology, it would have been necessary to write four books. *Being I* deals with extra-mental existence; *Being II* would have dealt with extra-mental essence; *Being III* with human co-existence; *Being IV* with human essence. This was the plan for publication. Only *Access to Being* and *Being I* were done. *Being I* is the formulation of the metaphysical theme from the abandonment of the mental limit. That is, the study of being as principle, which is precisely the theme that metaphysics deals with. Or, in other words, it is the theme of the first principles, which are three: the principle of identity—which is not the principle of unicity (unicity is the mental presence, which is abandoned in order to be able to formulate the principle of identity)—; the principle of causality; and the principle of non-contradiction. These are the three major existential themes of metaphysics. Metaphysics focuses on being as identity, on being as transcendental principle of causality, and on being as non-contradiction.

Meanwhile, the extra-mental essence (which would have been the theme of *Being II*) is precisely that essence whose being is principial; essence co-relative with created principial being. Insofar as essence is distinguished from being (this is the Thomistic real distinction of *essentia-esse*), extra-mental essence is dependent principiality; that is, predicamental principiality. For this reason, extra-mental essence are the four causes insofar as they are con-causal, or rather, in con-causality. The book *Being II* could have been published, but I am not going to do so since its contents are covered in Vol. IV of my *Course on the Theory of Knowledge*. In that book I set forth how the mental limit is abandoned in order to advert the first principles (the being that metaphysics deals with) and the predicamental causes (that is, the extra-mental essence as really distinct from extra-mental being). Thus, what remains to be explained are human co-existence (human being) and the essence of man, tasks that are taken up in another book that has not yet been published—*Transcendental Anthropology*, which brings together two of the previously mentioned volumes (*Being III* and *Being IV*).

I make reference to this program of publication because it is precisely the abandonment of the mental limit (or rather the abandonment of unicity) according to distinct modes that makes possible an approach to these four themes and, in particular, the thematic access to co-existence and human essence. It is a question of understanding how the abandonment of monism is the abandonment of unicity, and that this is the abandonment of the mental limit, which can be said to have four dimensions, and which can be done in four ways, each of which opens up a distinct theme.

In sum, the justification for transcendental anthropology is this: if the abandonment of the mental limit makes it possible to attain a dimension of being that is distinct from being as principle, then the being of man (which is not being as principle) can be attained. With another dimension, one also discovers being as principle: metaphysics. In this way the compatibility or the coordination of human being that anthropology studies with the being of metaphysics lies in that the unicity (unicity being the mental limit) can be abandoned in four ways. This is what we are trying to see—what abandonment of unicity is and why it can be done in four ways (which corresponds to four major themes): the being and essence that metaphysics and physics deal with and the being and the essence of man.

The articulation of anthropology with metaphysics lies in that they are two modes of abandoning the mental limit, that is, unicity. If the mental limit is abandoned in one way, the theme of physics appears; if in another way, the theme of metaphysics; in another, the theme of anthropology, which is twofold: human being and essence. In turn, the fact that anthropology is a transcendental expansion with respect to metaphysics ultimately takes place by virtue of the plurality of the dimensions of the abandonment of the "one." And, strictly speaking, the "one" is nothing more than the mental limit. The *mónon*, considered coherently, is only this: the mental presence. We will insist upon these questions in order to develop the approach for anthropology as expansion of the transcendental, and as distinct from metaphysics; that is, for the being of man as co-existence, because these formulations are equivalent.

Three basic theses regarding transcendental anthropology

It should be said that the proposed approach regarding a transcendental anthropology is quite difficult. Laying it out has the advantage of clarifying it a little. Having accepted that the approach is not incorrect, it is not wrong to find oneself faced with the difficult. It is good for the philosopher to get used to the difficulty of approaches.

First thesis. Thus far I have formulated three theses. The first states that one can speak of transcendental anthropology to the same extent that the discovery regarding human being is not reduced to metaphysics. Human being is studied in an indirect manner if it is assimilated into metaphysics. In this assimilation one loses what is truly unique to human being. Thus, speaking of transcendental anthropology is the same as proposing an expansion of the transcendental or, also, as maintaining the thesis that anthropology is not reducible to metaphysics. This does not entail disdain for metaphysics, nor a limitation, but rather simply a difference, a distinction. And it is that there is not only one sense of being. The sense of being that corresponds to man is not the same as the one that corresponds to the being that metaphysics studies.

Metaphysics is Greek in origin, and the Greeks did not consider man according to his strictest peculiarity. They understood him as nature, especially during the so-called anthropological era, which begins with the Sophists, after the crisis of the approaches of the pre-Socratic philosophers (who studied *physis*). And as a surpassing of the Sophists, the great Socratics propose the notion of human *physis*, of man's nature. For this reason, it can be said that Greek anthropology is the consideration of man as *physis*. But this is not yet the study of man as *esse*, as being; it is not yet the study of human being.

On the other hand, the study of human being is fitting within the Christian approach. Within this approach one discovers the being of man: in Christianity the human being is not only nature, but also person; and the person implies being. Man is a personal being. To be a person is not *physis*, nor is it the being that metaphysics deals with. Is a metaphysical formulation of the notion of person possible? As I see it, this formulation presents difficulties. Clearly, the person is a theological theme, but theology is not philosophy. In speculative theology one speaks of the divine Persons when studying the Trinity, of the Person of Christ with two natures (which also makes it clear that person is distinct from nature), etc. Man can also be proposed as person from within theology. But I think that the being of man as person can be a philosophical theme in itself.

As I see it, the study of man as personal being also belongs to philosophy. And that would be the transcendental anthropology that I propose, which, according to my thought, is not metaphysics. Why? Because "metaphysics" means the trans-physical—that which is beyond the physical. First Philosophy (which is the strictly Aristotelian name, and not metaphysics) is, in turn, the study of what is first and, therefore, of being as principle, of a sense of being that is the principial sense. Now, must this notion be considered as surpassed? No. Metaphysics continues to have a perfectly real theme. It cannot be said that it is past or historical. The principial or grounding sense of being is undeniable. Therefore, metaphysics is neither eliminated nor substituted. But the person is not a principle, nor a ground. It is another sense of being. Or, in other words, by proposing the expansion of the transcendental (with anthropology), metaphysics is deprived of its character of monopoly with respect to the theme of being. Being need not belong only to metaphysics, which (as has been suggested) studies being as ground or principle. But there is a being, a sense of being, that is not this. It is the person. The sense of being as person is also radical, but (it seems to me) the radicality should not be likened to the notion of ground.

An indication that the personal sense of being cannot be assimilated to the being of being as ground is that otherwise it would be impossible to speak of the divine Persons because, then how would the Unity and Trinity of God be made compatible? If the Unity and the Trinity had the same sense, it would seem to me that there is a contradiction. But this is only a suggestion regarding how one could go about formulating the approach.

Something similar can be seen in man, although in a different way. Personal being is the "who" or "each one". In contrast, human nature is, as it were, that which is common. All men are of the same nature, but we are not all the same person. This is obvious. To the point that if the notion of person is applied as something common, then it is not truly designative of human being. If "person" is taken as a common term, then we are all "*that*" which is called *person*: I am person, you are person, he is person; person is predicated, and one loses sight that the person is the "who", that is, that which is irreducible to what is common (or to the general or to the universal) through co-existing. The person that I am is distinguished from the person that you are: we are irreducible. To speak of person in a common way, or in a general sense, is a reduction. No one is the person that the other is, because in that case she would not co-exist. Human nature can certainly be considered as universal; but not the person, because, in intimate coherence with the irreducible difference of the person, persons co-exist. Person points to many meanings, all of which are transcendental; but it means, above all, irreducibility, that is, *who*. *Who* is irreducible co-existing. One can speak of "who" as a universal; but its consideration as a universal is not the person (but rather, in any case, the "personality"; but the personality does not exist). For this reason, it is necessary to seek to go further, or to take note of the insufficiency that the Greek approach has when dealing with the person. Person is that which is most dignified, says Thomas Aquinas. But then unity is not superior to it. Therefore it is useless to consider it as a universal. Since we think in terms of the universal, we can transpose the notion of person to the universal, that is, understand it as a concept. But we have to realize that this is not so—the person is not a universal, because by virtue of its co-existing, the one is not superior to it. One solitary person is absolutely impossible.

In God, says Thomas Aquinas, the Persons are described as relations of opposition. The Father is not the Son; the Son is not the Father, etc. This is precisely what is distinct in God, as it were. Thus, the opposition of relations (moreover, of subsistent relations, since they are Persons) can be compatible with the divine identity or simplicity. Of these subsistent relations one is the Father, another the Son and another the Holy Spirit. It would not be right to speak of the divine personality, but rather of divine Persons; and each one is Person. The Who that is. Three in God is transcendental.

Man is also person. Personal being means who. Who means co-existing. Metaphysics sometimes functions in general or with universal concepts. It speaks, for example, of the universal concept of entity. Fine; but to understand the person as a universal is not correct. Can it be done? Yes, but for linguistic requirements. Strictly speaking, "each" person is irreducible. Therefore, neither a general nor a universal idea is enough. It would be necessary to say the person "so-and-so" and the person "what's his name"; and "so-and-so" and "what's his name" point to the radicality of the person. Why? Well, precisely because of the consideration of "who"; not because of the consideration of the singularity nor because the universals are not real, etc. These are approaches that address metaphysical or gnoseological concerns. It cannot be said that an individual cat is a person. The singular cat is not a "who": that is the question. And neither is it correct to say that the person is an individual. Man is neither singular nor a universal, but rather person, that is, completely irreducible. Person does not mean *unum in multis*, but rather the radically superior.

This puts forth the first thesis, according to which the being that transcendental anthropology studies is not the being that metaphysics deals with. Man is a distinct being. And we can describe this sense of being like this: it is personal being. Personal being belongs to man. Personal being does not belong to being in the grounding sense. When something like a ground or a cause is understood, it is not for this reason understood as person. It is not by understanding grounding being that one understands the person. On the other hand, human being is either understood as person or it is not understood; or it is understood indirectly or by extrapolation.

Thus, it seems to me that transcendental anthropology is justified. It can still, however, be clarified from other points of view, which I will attempt to develop. But this is sufficient for a presentation of the first thesis (speaking of transcendental anthropology implies an expansion of the transcendental). The person is transcendental in a way different from how transcendentals are spoken of in metaphysics, especially starting from the Middle Ages.

Second thesis. The second thesis is as follows: so that the expansion of the transcendental with anthropology does not entail a disparagement or disqualification of metaphysics, and at the same time that it sufficiently establish the difference, it is said that human being should not be called existence, but rather co-existence. The being that metaphysics studies is called existential, without being incorrect. Some argue that it is not correct to call the *actus essendi* existence, because existing is empirical. I do not accept this. The being that metaphysics deals with is being as existence, because in order to be ground it must exist—it cannot be ground without existing, no matter how important it is to clarify the term existence; but this is not the case at the moment and it is a metaphysical theme that I deal with in *Being I*.

It can be said that the being that metaphysics studies is convertible with existence. But the being that anthropology studies is not convertible, because it is *co-existence*. This is consistent above all with the expansion of the transcendental. Because this expansion is not a mere generalization, nor a higher universal (in spite of the fact that it is often said that the transcendental is the most universal); with the expansion of the transcendental it is not a question of the superuniversal, but of something else. The person is not universal. Precisely because of this, the being that transcendental anthropology deals with is not equivalent to existence; it is not called existence, but rather co-existence. And this is coherent with the expansion. Precisely because it is co-existence, it takes nothing away from existence. There is no co-existence without existence. For this reason. it is totally compatible with existence; it has no quarrel with existence, it does not exclude it. Human co-existing requires the existing with which it co-exists, although existing is not co-existing. Man co-exists with being in the grounding sense even though being ground is not co-existing (and without co-existing being exhausted in this). Co-existing is, so to speak, being expanded on the inside: intimacy, being as sphere-in-which.

For this reason, the word "expansion" can be proposed in the manner indicated. It is not, shall we say, a purely methodological designation, but rather it points to the theme itself, because the expansion is co-existence. That is, the expansion has to refer to itself. And to refer the expansion of being to being has to do with "being-with" or co-existing: co-being; accompanying being, so to speak (all these are indicative expressions). And co-existing is characteristic of the person.

Therefore, although the person is irreducible, it signifies co-existence. In God, this is clear; but also in man. And certainly, it is not said that animals co-exist. Persons co-exist. Consequently, human being, co-existence does not signify *mónon*, "one". Or, in other words, one solitary person makes no sense. Persons are irreducible; but irreducibility does not signify solitary person. One solitary person is impossible. On the one hand, persons co-exist with that which is not co-existence, that is, with grounding being. But they also co-exist with each other: there is personal co-existence. The irreducibility of the person is not isolating; it is not separation. For this reason, neither does person signify substance. Substance is that which is separated; but the separated does not co-exist; rather, it is isolated. Substances exist each one on its own; they exist, but they do not co-exist. Leibniz carried this to its ultimate consequences with his idea of the monad. But the person is neither a monad, nor is without windows.

All of the above seems clear, although it is a subject that needs to be always explored more so that it does not remain just a presentation or announcement (like Nietzsche's superman). It involves a theory of personal being. And this is, above all, transcendental anthropology. It can also be theology, but before that it is philosophy.

At the same time, it is an approach that also opens up a way to access God that is distinct from the one that metaphysics makes possible—an anthropological access to God. Metaphysics does, indeed, develop ways to access God. These are the five Thomistic ways, but they are distinct from the access to God through anthropology. The metaphysical ways terminate in God as principle: God as prime mover, as first cause, as necessary being on which contingent beings depend, God as the first in the order of the participation of pure perfections, and God as intelligence on which order depends. In all these ways, God is understood as first. Thus,

Thomas Aquinas states: we conclude in the prime mover, which we call God; we conclude in the first cause, which we call God, etc. But this is so because one arrives at God from the sense of being as principle. And it is obvious that the principial sense of being corresponds to God. God, however, is not exhausted by being a principle. Because personal being, co-existing, can also be said of God. Is a sixth metaphysical way achieved in this way? No, because in anthropology God is not considered as principle or as cause. God is the creator of the human person, but being creator of the person does not mean being cause of the person. Although this too will be justified later.

In any case, this can be said in another way: creating does not always mean the same thing. Why? Because it depends on the being that is created, since personal being is distinct from grounding being. Thomas Aquinas says that being is divided into two: created and uncreated. It can be added that the creature is also divided into two. Thus, creation will be distinct for these two creatures. Moreover, this is the only approach that permits transcendental freedom. In the order of grounding, there is room for nothing but a grounded freedom, which presents an enormous problem, and is not a transcendental freedom, but rather a secondary freedom. In the end it is an impossible freedom. Nevertheless, one can, in a certain way, speak of a more or less grounded freedom, at least with regard to what is called *motive*. But in this sense, freedom is not transcendental.

In what sense is freedom transcendental? As personal freedom. But in this case, what does freedom mean? For now, let us point out that it is a new sense of freedom, and it is found in the order of human *esse*, of personal being, and not in the order of the nature of man, in which there is also freedom, or, better, to which freedom *extends*. And thus, insofar as it is extended to nature, it can be considered by metaphysics, although it always gives rise to very difficult problems. First of all, a certain incompatibility, because a grounded freedom is not, properly speaking, freedom, or it will be so secondarily or partially. For this reason, freedom has to be personal. If it is transcendental, if it is in the order of *esse*, then this *esse* has to be the person and not the ground. But then it is not susceptible to metaphysical consideration. For this reason, it has to be equivalent to co-existing and be distinguished from the ground. Freedom and ground are compatible. Freedom and ground do not arise from each other, if they are understood properly. If freedom is either placed along the line of ground or is grounded, then it is either not free or is so precariously; or, if it is ungrounded, one arrives at Ockham (arbitrariness) or at Sartre (the absurd). Either a capricious will or nonsense.

Now, being free does not mean lacking a ground, but rather a sense of being that is distinct from the ground, which is not in the line of the ground: not as ground, nor as grounded or ungrounded. Would it be fitting to establish this distinction? Yes, although it is not necessary, because theology already makes reference to the person, and that might be enough. Through Revelation we know that freedom is the freedom with which Christ freed us, etc. For this reason, I say that transcendental anthropology is not necessary, although it is highly fitting and timely, among other things because it resolves the question of arbitrariness and the absurd.

And it is because freedom on the plane of co-existence is not arbitrary; it cannot be so. In contrast, freedom in the order of the ground is either little freedom or an absurd freedom (in the Sartrean sense). Sartre refers to this distinction in *Being and Nothingness*: entity, as *en soi*, on the one hand, and, on the other hand, freedom as nothingness or *pour soi*. But freedom is co-existence, not nothingness.

In any event, modern philosophy has tried to understand freedom as transcendental, and effectively speaks of transcendental freedom. Kant, for example, characterizes his philosophy as transcendental (although this sense of the transcendental is not classical). For him (it can be said), freedom is a transcendental (in the sense that he understands it) since it is the *ratio essendi* of the categorical imperative. The categorical imperative is transcendental, that is, absolutely imperative—a pure imperative, not conditioned, precisely because the subject is free. But Kant continues thinking in terms of ground, because freedom then grounds the categorical imperative. In any case, freedom already appears as such, as transcendental, in Kant, although this character is denied, since when he speaks of *ratio essendi* and *ratio cognoscendi*, he thinks about it in the grounding sense. The Kantian sense of the transcendental is not classical, but it is *symmetric* with the classical.

Thus, transcendental freedom has to be thought of in terms of co-existence and not in terms of grounding. In the co-existential order one should not speak of grounding. The "co existents" do not ground one another; they are something higher or more elevated than the ground. An example could help here: *genitum non factum*, the Creed says of the Son. This means that the Father is not the cause of the Son. He is the Father of the Son, but not his cause. In God, internally, there is no causality. Divine causality is *ad extra*. All the more reason to say that there is a sense of being that is not in the order of causality or of grounding. If we call this sense of being being-with or co-existence, then it is clear, on the one hand, that co-existing is compatible with being; on the other hand, it is clear that there is neither a relation of grounding in the co-existence of persons with each other, nor of persons with respect to the universe. And only for this reason can it be said that all men are equal. Or that the human person does not proceed from his parents, but rather is directly created by God. This is said of the soul, but with much more reason it must be said of the person.

Among the philosophers who have spoken about transcendental freedom, we can point to Karl Jaspers and Martin Heidegger. In *Von Wesen des Grundes*, a work from the *Being and Time* cycle, Heidegger says that freedom is ground: ground without ground, *Abgrund*. For Jaspers, freedom is also assimilated to the ground. For this reason, in neither of these authors is transcendental freedom convertible with co-existence. Moreover, they demand freedom as autonomy, but with respect to the ground, more or less following the Kantian line of thought.

In sum, modern philosophy places great importance on freedom. Descartes already argued that what is most like God, and what is most important in man is freedom: free will. But he does not interpret free will in the order of co-existence; or rather, it is not a personal freedom. And for this reason, modern philosophy falls into inconsistency here.

However, with regard to this point, it is better to correct modern philosophy rather than refute it, that is, to point out that these philosophers attempt to formulate notions that remained unexplored, even though they were not successful. Even then, this attempt is not useless: it points to a legitimate issue, although it addresses it incorrectly. It is always the case that when one can salvage something that others have thought, then it should be done. With regard to the history of philosophy, the *in peius* interpretation must be rejected. No author, or better, no system, thesis, or formulated philosophical theory should be interpreted pejoratively, because something true will never be lacking, and it is important to save what it vaguely perceived. For this reason, one must always deal with it *in melius*: understanding by improving upon. If the author cannot give more of himself, it is necessary to at least to salvage what he truly catches a glimpse of. In this case, that freedom does not fit within a solely grounding approach, or that it is a theme to be studied. And instead of saying that he was wrong, it seems better to continue forward. This is why I say transcendental freedom is co-existential. And that is what modern philosophy did not see. Freedom is a co-existential transcendental, not an existential one. Thus, it is not a question of "existentialism", but rather, if you will, of a "co-existentialism". And this is because, from this proposal, the very designation "existential" is bad.

Thus, this is the second thesis: that the expansion of the transcendental is coherent if this expansion is in terms of *being-*

with or *co-existence*, and not existence. Personal co-existence and grounding existence are thus distinguished from each other. This must be correctly understood because, since there is a strong tendency in man to think causally (given that he always attempts to discover something regarding the ground or principle), it is important to distance oneself from this inclination when taking up the subject matter of transcendental anthropology. And this is precisely what modern philosophy does not achieve.

The tendency to think causally is so strong, among other reasons, because man is in the universe and co-exists with it, constructing the world. He is not a being-in-the-world (*in-der-Welt-Sein*), as Heidegger says, but rather *co-exists in the world*. And even less, it is clear, is he an intracosmic being. The person transcends the universe. But his transcending it does not mean that he is the ground of the universe. He clearly is not. It means that he transcends it adding the "with" to the universe, adding co-existence to existence.

I insist. Since we tend to seek why things are, and our investigation is normally directed toward the ground, this approach (co-existing is not the same as existing, and is not in the order of grounding) can seem strange, especially if it is also argued that co-existing is a sense of being that is superior to existing and to the ground. Because, ever since antiquity, we consider the ground as higher. Metaphysically this is true: what is first in the order of grounding is the highest—the first principle. This (*De primo principio*) has been dealt with by metaphysicians. And for this reason it can seem to us that the first principle is the culmination of being. However, co-existing is more than being first principle. And this may seem a bit forced to our minds, which long to know what is first. But, why does it not long to know what is most intimate? The first principle, if it really is first, is neither the highest, nor the most intimate. The most intimate is the person, and the person is no less radical than the ground; except that its radicality is not grounding.

Now then, what is the radicality that is more radical than grounding? In being is there something more than grounding? Yes. It is a conviction that sometimes appears and which frequently returns. It is that which is expressed in the thesis that *bonum est diffusivum sui* (the good is diffusive of itself). Certainly, that the *bonum* is *diffusivum sui* ultimately retains something reminiscent of grounding, because in reality it is thought of in terms of degradation. That the good is diffusive of itself points to the ground insofar as it gives rise to what is derived, which is precisely the termination of the diffusion.

However, this being the good diffusive of itself implies something like a bestowal [*otorgar*], a benevolence; and inasmuch as there is benevolence we are already beyond the ground. Thus, the expression *bonum diffusivum sui*, elicits, so to say, the consideration of the *bonum* as ground and as bestower [*otorgante*]. But as bestowing, the good is no longer exactly ground.

This also appears in Thomas Aquinas. When he says that God is the efficient cause of the creature, it is clear that he is understanding it in the order of grounding. But when he says *creatio est donatio essendi*, this is no longer understood in the grounding order. He expands the causal consideration. When something is gifted, it is not grounded, it is not caused; something more than grounding is done. That is, being is given—it is not caused, nor made, but rather given. What is more characteristic of creation: making being or giving being? (Understood correctly: as *ex nihilo sui et subjecti*, or rather, without a subject. Here we also find the suggestion that the notion of substance is not radical. What is separated is not primary, because this *ex nihilo* is *ex nihilo substantiae*. There can be no matter, nor preexisting subject: nothing previous). But *facere extra nihilum* is not the same as giving being *extra nihilum*. Giving being is higher than making it (*ex nihilo*). The gift-vision of creation is more than artisanal. What is more properly creating: grounding or giving? Giving; and insofar as it is given, we are already in the order of co-existence.

These observations are not intended to downplay the importance of the notion of grounding. Moreover, I say that this notion is legitimate. It is a sense of being. There is a creature that is grounded, and this creature is precisely that which exists, that which is in the order of the first principles. But one can see that there is another sense of being that is not existential and which, therefore, is not in the order of grounding—it is higher. This sense of being is that which is fitting to the notion of person, since it must be thought like this: personal being is co-existential.

And the underlying reason for this is seen when one understands to what extent the person is incompatible with monism. Because the notion of one solitary person is absolutely incoherent. Moreover, one solitary person would be pure tragedy. For this reason, the worst thing that could happen to a human being is to isolate itself or to become arrogant. Selfishness and pride are contrary to gift-being. For this reason, it is not right to say that man is merely a subject. We have to go from the subject to the I. And from the I to the person. Because neither is it enough to say that man is an I. This leads to "egotism"—in no way self-person (self-conscience), but rather co-existence. The modern subject is faced, speculatively, with the representation; it isolates itself from anyone else by entangling itself with the problem of certainty. No modern philosopher has resolved the question of intersubjectivity.

Moreover, this is consistent with the fact that God cannot be a uni-personal being: he is tri-personal. If God were not trinitarian, if he were *mónon*, then tragedy would be in God Himself. Who proposed that tragedy is to be found within God? Nietzsche. He is not an atheist, but rather a tragic theist. Dionysius is the god of his tragic theism. An atheological theism, so to say, because Dionysius himself is not susceptible to the *logos*, because he is not logical. In the dualism with which Nietzsche's philosophy begins and which never ceases to be present in it, the *logos* belongs to Apollo, but not to Dionysius. When *Zarathustra* begins to consider the problem of eternity, he approaches it as the eternal return of the same, and so encounters the divinity, understands it as Dionysius and, therefore, as tragic: Dionysius is alone, and plays by himself. Insofar as one accepts the monism of the person (alone or by itself), then the ontic is tragic. And this is so because it cannot co-exist with its equal, in such a way that it becomes lost, and leads to nothingness. For this reason, nothingness is forever, says Nietzsche. This is the direction that his nihilism goes. In Nietzsche there is something like a renewed vital exuberance that is grounding or principial, but not personal—it is full of passion, but it is not personal. For this reason tragedy and pain are inserted into it. "Deep is the pain", he says, and "deep is the pleasure". This division is also found in Dionysius, who is the tragic interpretation of the divinity. But this interpretation is absurd. But, why does he think this way? Because Nietzsche does not attain co-existence. He puts it this way: a sun cannot warm another sun; if what is highest is plural, then it does not admit co-existence. A sun is cold for another; each one is isolated. But then there can only be compassion, the ontological descent. Zarathustra comes down the mountain.

Thus, this is the second thesis: the expansion of the transcendental is, so to speak, insistent; and therefore is co-existence. This implies a "with respect to" that is intrinsic. In God it is the subsistent relation. It is a respective being, a being that cannot be uni-personal.

Third thesis. It states that in order to study the being of man it is necessary to realize that being man is superior to unicity. I initially formulated this thesis making reference to earlier works of mine, but not independently. Metaphysically, unicity is the *mónon*—the notion of the "one", which leads to pantheism; the totality of the "one", the "one" totality. Now, the approach of the transcendental expansion requires abandoning the "one". I usually say that the method for arriving at personal being is the abandonment of unicity. This obliges us to establish precisely what unicity means or, so to say, where it is given and where it is.

Now, unicity is not the ground. It is not a question of monism of the ontological or grounding type. Unicity is the descriptive characteristic of the intellectual operation. This is why I started speaking about mental operations.

This thesis also involves difficulties. With what has been said, it seems to me that the difficulties of the first two theses are to some extent controlled. The being that the expansion of the transcendental studies is being-with, the person, hence it cannot be only one—that would be an ontological tragedy. And an ontological tragedy is impossible—the ultimate, the most important, cannot be the tragic. Tragedy can appear in human life because man sins precisely because of the decoupling of co-existing, by wanting to not co-exist. Original sin is a sin against co-existence. It is wanting to live alone—to disobey God and act without Him by breaking community with God. And he who speaks of community speaks of co-existence; from the point of view of the person, community means co-existing.

The third thesis states: the person is superior to unicity and, therefore, if there is a methodology for anthropology, it will be the way by which we discover, starting from unicity, the superiority of the person. Thus, the first thing is to attempt to say what, strictly speaking, unicity means. And I state: "the only one" that means "unicity" is the mental presence. That is, that cognitive act of the intelligence that possesses an object: the immanent operation. The immanent operation is well described as the notion of unicity.

Accordingly, the approach, the way or method by which one can develop and establish the thematic of transcendental anthropology is the abandonment of the mental limit—the abandonment of unicity. Because unicity means limit. It is obvious by this equivalence—presence is equivalent to unicity; and presence is equivalent to limit. If it is mental presence or unicity, then the limit will be the mental limit. And this must be so, because operative knowledge is the lowest among the hierarchy of the acts of knowledge.

Knowledge is always in act. But intellectual operating, that is, the cognitive act that is an operation, is the least of those acts. There is also a hierarchy in operative knowledge: seeing is lower than abstracting, and abstracting is lower than conceiving, etc. In the intellectual order, the lowest acts are the intellectual operations. Above them are the other intellectual acts.

Now, the method by virtue of which one can arrive at the being of man (it seems to me and thus I propose it) is, first of all, to discover, to reveal, or to detect that the operation as mental presence is unicity and limit; and, having detected this, to abandon it. Detecting the limit makes abandoning it possible, and by abandoning the limit I can arrive at a wider thematic, one theme of which is precisely the *esse* of man, that is, co-existence.

What I call the detecting of the mental limit in conditions for abandoning it and, therefore, in such a way that superior cognitive acts come into play, is the method that permits the discovery of and access to four major themes: two metaphysical and two anthropological. For this reason, I say that the abandonment of the mental limit has four major dimensions or, in other words, that it can be done along four directions. Let us see if I present this in a coherent way.

The abandonment of the limit and some precedents

The mental limit is intellectual operation as lowest cognitive act of the intelligence. It can be detected; and, upon being detected, be abandoned (or to use a less adequate phrase, be surpassed. I prefer not to use the notion of surpassing). Its abandonment opens up a wider thematic, which corresponds to intellectual acts that are superior to operations. This abandonment can be done in four ways, for which reason I speak of four dimensions of the abandonment of the mental limit that correspond to four major themes:

extra-mental existence, which is the theme of metaphysics; extra-mental essence, which a physical-metaphysical theme; human existence, which I call co-existence; and human essence, which I call (we will see later why) availing-of [*disponer*].

Why four themes? First, because it is by these four ways that the abandonment of the limit is carried out. But also, from another point of view, because this is the way to link the themes of metaphysics and physics, as well as the anthropological themes, with the philosophical discovery of Thomas Aquinas. That is, *this is a new exposition of the real distinction of* essentia *and* esse. The real distinction between essence and act of being is characteristic of every creature, that which distinguishes it from God. This thesis is the summit of Thomism and, therefore, of classical philosophy. Classical philosophy culminates in this thesis: essence and *esse* are really distinct *in creatis*.

Now, since the being of man is created and is distinct from extra-mental existence (which is also created), there are two senses of creation: the grounding and the co-existential (or strictly speaking, gifting [*donal*]). The creation of man is not the grounding sense of creation, but rather that which is properly gifting. Thus, there is also a difference between the real distinction of the essence of man and human being and the real distinction *essentia-esse* in the grounding creature. The real distinction is discovered in its most radical sense if it is dealt with in metaphysics and also in anthropology; in this way they are adverted and accessed in their distinction by going beyond the operation—knowing something more than what operation knows. In sum, the main precedent of the proposed approach is the real distinction *essentia-esse* as set forth by Thomas Aquinas. I propose a new exposition that focuses on the distinction between human being (and her essence) and the being of the universe and its physical essence. In this way better understanding of both senses of being and of essence is achieved, one that is superior to what operations know.

And what do operations know? Objects. Thus, transcendental knowledge, strictly speaking, must be trans-objective. Trans-objective because it is reached by abandoning the mental limit, with acts that are superior to operations. Upon abandoning the operation, it is no longer objects that are known, but more than objects. And this trans-objective knowledge is fourfold.

In addition to this, the proposal of trans-objective knowledge, that is, of "surpassing" objective thought, has frequently been formulated throughout the history of philosophy. In Plato, for example. When he says that the *pantelôs ón*, that is, the fullness of reality is the good and that the good is beyond the ideas, he is pointing to the trans-ideal or trans-objective. The good is trans-objective or trans-ideal. This is repeated in a more radical way (although also in a confused way) in Plotinus. Furthermore, precisely because of the influence of Platonism and of Neo-platonism, this is also present in medieval philosophy. For example, when Thomas Aquinas speaks of knowledge by connaturality, which is not objective.

For its part, in modern philosophy the notion of trans-objectivity has at times been formulated. Occasionally, under the form of a vigorous rejection of objective knowledge, something that I do not share because objective knowledge is intentional and is valid, even though it is not a superior one. Others state that objective knowledge is the only type of knowledge, but that with it, not everything can be known. Thus, appeal must be made to the emotional, as a kind of intuition, such as Max Scheler's emotive intuition of values, or as empathy, etc. Some moderns speak of the trans-objective in the sense of the irrational. The trans-objective can be reached in voluntarism. The God of Ockham is certainly not objective; it is not possible to speak objectively of God because Ockham has rejected objectivizations, the suppositional value of ideas. God is arbitrary will, and this is obviously irrational. Irrationalism is often times a rejection of objective knowledge. Others, like Jaspers, speak of the trans-objective in the sense of a transcending or going beyond. Jaspers, however, does not control the way this is done.

My proposal is a way of controlling trans-objective knowledge. If the limit is detected, it is abandoned, that is, trans-objectifying is made possible, since the limit is the presence of objects. If I abandon the presence, I no longer objectivize. But there is control, since it does not entail that I fall into the irrational, nor that I know nothing, but rather that I control intellectual acts that are superior to operations.

Heidegger also refers to the trans-objective in the sense that for him the objective is (so to say) an uncoupling of what is known as ordered to existential understanding, the meaning of being, and to what he calls pre-understanding: *Vor-begriff*, *Vor-haben*. This, he says, is the same as human existing. But for Heidegger, man is existence, not co-existence, despite his reference to *Mit-sein*, which he does not sufficiently develop. Knowing would be a mode of man's existing—man knows what is called being by being. And therefore, if it is by being that what is called being is known, if knowledge coincides with existence, then it is beyond the object, because the object would be that which is represented. It is there in front, but it is not attained by a cognitive impulse that is in solidarity with, and comes from, existence itself. For this reason, it can be said that in Heidegger objectivism is considered an improper way of knowing.

Even for Hegel the knowledge of the absolute is not merely objective, but rather objective-subjective. That is how he himself expresses it. In any case, in my view, this is not a proposal of trans-objectivity that is as clear as the one found in Plato when he speaks of the good, or in existential authors influenced by Kierkegaard, whose approach would also be an attempt at trans-objectivization.

What is certain is that the topic that objective knowledge is not the highest or that there is something superior to it, appears in the history of philosophy and is frequently associated with the speculative version of the object. Its

rejection leads to accepting that what is superior in life is
wanting or emotions, that is, something irrational. This is also
in Nietzsche, when he argues that objective truth is a concern
for man, but not for the superman. It is also clear that the
question appears throughout the history of philosophy without
intellectual control. It is precisely this control that I propose—
the limitation of objective knowledge is detected by intellectual
acts that are superior to the immanent operation. Without
these superior acts, the limitation of objective knowledge
would not be noticed in any way. Therefore, it is incorrect to
hold that man only knows objectively and that in order to rise
to the consideration of the human one must leave knowledge
behind. This illustrates the thesis that in order to attain human
being (in order to arrive at it), it is necessary to abandon the
mental limit. But it must be kept well in mind that abandoning
the mental limit does not only permit attaining human
existence and the essence of man. If human being is equivalent
to co-existence, attaining it must also allow access to existence
and to extra-mental essence, that is, to the themes of
metaphysics and physics-metaphysics.

By establishing these four dimensions one also sees that
anthropology is not reducible to metaphysics and that,
moreover, it is not isolated from it since both anthropology as
well as metaphysics (as I understand them) are developments
of that important thesis about the creature which is the real
distinction between being and essence. Thus, it is possible to
access the metaphysical thematic from the perspective of the
real distinction in this way—by the abandonment of the limit.
The anthropological thematic is an expansion.

Four thematic areas

I will now briefly present, or outline, these four major
thematic areas.

How is the limit abandoned in order to advert [*advertir*]
extra-mental existence? The limit is abandoned (that is, the

operation) and one passes on to a superior act, which is the habit of the first principles. Among other things, this notion, that of the habit of the first principles, is entirely classical. However, something must be added to the classical meaning of this notion: the knowledge of the first principles (which is properly speaking habitual) is a way of abandoning the limit, because the habit is another intellectual act, one that is superior to operations. The habit of the first principles is the knowledge of being in the grounding sense. For this reason, this habit is that abandonment of the mental limit according to which metaphysics is rigorously known in an axiomatic way. Since the first principles are axioms, they are the way to axiomatically formulate the knowledge of the ground, and this is the best way to approach metaphysics, since in this manner the created and uncreated acts of being are clearly distinguished. Neither of them is the Aristotelian *entelékheia*, which is a sense of act that must be corrected because it is not transcendental, and, also, because the assistance of the ground, being intrinsic, cannot be actual (the actual is the object, the knowledge of which is abandoned). Note that Aristotle does not say that God is *entelékheia*; he calls him *energeía*, *nóesis noéseos nóesis*. But this designation is not accurate either, since the cognitive operation is the mental limit and does not know itself; but it is highly significant. In the end, Aristotle is not a philosopher of substance. His two senses of act—*enérgeia* and *entelékheia*—, the first entirely correct, have to be distinguished from the Thomistic act of being. I call the act of being-created of the universe *persistence*, and I describe it as beginning that neither ceases nor is followed. It is the first principle of non-contradiction. I call the divine act of being *Origin*. It is the first principle of identity.

How is the extra-mental essence known upon abandoning the limit? In the way I call *explicitation* [*explicitación*]. The formulation of the explicitation is the study of the predicamental order. To see, to find the predicamental order, is to know the causes. The explicitation is also a kind of abandonment of the mental limit, which I call *tension* [*pugna*] of the operation with the first predicamental principles or

40

devolution of the object to reality. The causes are found or encountered, but not possessed by the operation; rather, it is in tension with them. The tension is made possible by maintaining the manifestation of the mental presence by habits that are inferior to the habit of the first principles. Since the mental presence is a priority, an act, but neither transcendent nor physical, it is in tension with, or confronts, the physical causes.

The essence is known by explicitating all the causes inasmuch as they are con-causes (the causes are *ad invicem*). Extra-mental existence is adverted; the extra-mental essence (that is, the order of the causes) is found, is encountered, or is contemplated. And encountering the causes is equivalent to explicitating. Furthermore, since the causes are con-causal (*ad invicem*), it is possible to explicitate not only the entire quadruple con-causality (which is the extra-mental essence), but also triple con-causalities and the double or hylomorphic con-causality. Thus, notions of physical movement, substance, and nature that are inferior to the extra-mental essence are found. The extra-mental essence is described as the fulfilled unity of order, but the order is not entirely fulfilled because this fulfillment is carried out by distinct causes. For this reason, the extra-mental essence is potency and is distinguished from the act of being.

In turn, in the abandonment of the limit, human existence is known by *attaining it* [*alcanzándola*]. Human co-existence is not adverted nor is found, but rather is attained. To attain is to arrive at what I call *additionally* [*además*]*. To attain is to attain the character of "additionally". Because if it is a question of co-existence, that is, of an expansion of the transcendental order, and, on the other hand, if co-existence is, at the same time, the most intimate or irreducible (not only the most proper), then it is known only to the extent that it is attained. In contrast, it cannot really be said that extra-mental existence is attained, but rather that it is adverted (the extra-mental

---

* *Además* can be translated also as beyond, evermore, furthermore, being more or besides (note of the translators).

essence is encountered, is found), because the extra-mental is distinguished from the *sphere* of the person. But the person is known if it is attained.

If the abandonment of the mental allows *me* to know *my* co-existence, then I attain it, accompanying it—strictly speaking, I do not know *it*, since being a human person means attaining being (the human person is created, not the originating identity). Attaining being denotes accompanying, not *terminus* (being is not a result). Neither does the human person mean *one-and-the-same*, since the same is the object that is thought. Attaining accompanying being, co-existing, is simply more than coming to be, and can be described as *future without defuturization*. The future is denoted by attaining: the non defuturization, by not coming to be, which is superfluous with regard to accompanying. In accordance with this, the person is open intimacy. And this is light, transcendental freedom. Essential freedom is intimately assisted; it assents. To assent is to avail-of. In accordance with the potentiality of the essence of man (which is really distinct from the act of human being) essential freedom connects with the habitual manifestation.

Now, within this methodological line, human co-existence is described as what I call the character of *additionally*. This is coherent, but not easy to present, and at first glance seems like a merely linguistic artifice, since "additionally" is an adverb. What does it mean that human co-existence is an adverb? In a certain way, Eckhart already points to it, when he says that the Son of God is the Verb [*Verbo*] and man is the adverb[2]. The adverb exists with the verb. And what creature co-exists with respect to the Verb? I call it "additionally" insofar as no creature adds anything to God, in such a way that *additionally* redounds upon the creature—she attains co-existing without being added, but rather *extra nihilum*. It is possible, therefore, to distinguish two senses of this adverb. *Additionally*, firstly, is overflow [*sobrar*] with respect to the operation: *the pure non-*

---

2 Note that, in this sense, "additionally" (*además*) is the adverb that expresses pure adverbility.

exhausting itself when operatively knowing; this is the first meaning of additionally. For this reason, it can also be said that habit is additionally to the operation. Nevertheless, the habit is distinguished from the additionally *extra nihilum*—it is superior to the operation, not caused by the operation, but rather is the light of the *intellectus ut actus* that manifests it. It is precisely this light that is human co-existence[3]. The character of *additionally* of human co-existence has to be (shall we say) the character of the entire total overflowing of the created intellectual light with respect to the unicity of the limit, that is, with respect to operating. By being *extra nihilum* act, it is also an act that is really distinct from the essence of man (or an act that is more distinct from God than from nothingness, and an act more distinct from nothingness than from essence. Inasmuch as it is distinct from nothingness, it is additionally-act or co-existence. Inasmuch as distinct from essence, it illuminates it. The essence of man is habitual manifestation).

Finally, the abandonment of the mental limit that allows access to the essence of man is what I call *detention* [*detención*]. To be detained in the limit is its habitual manifestation. Or, if one will, the manner by which one passes from the limit to the habits. Because it is in the habits where the nature of man is essence. The extra-mental essence is distinguished from physical natures because the former is the quadruple con-causality, while the latter are triple con-causalities. Thus, the extra-mental essence adds the unity of order (that is, the final cause) to natures. For this reason, the extra-mental essence is described as the perfection of natures. This perfection is the physical universe[4]. For its part, the essence of man is the perfection of his nature, but this perfection is habitual, and not the final cause (the habits are not physical causes). The distinction between extra-mental essence and the essence of man is necessary if the act of human being is not a first principle (in accordance with the proposed expansion of the

---

3   The *intellectus ut actus*, that is, the Aristotelian agent intellect, is a personal transcendental in anthropology.

4   As essence, the physical universe is distinct from its act of being, which is persistence, a first principle, as pointed out earlier.

transcendental). The essence of man is the intrinsic perfection of a nature procured by the co-existential act of being. This perfection is habitual, and, therefore, is described as *to-avail-of* [*disponer*]. Considered from the essence, the operations that man exercises are dispositive modalities that correspond to that which is available [*lo disponible*]. To-avail-of [*disponer*] should not be confused with that which is available [*lo disponible*]. Moral duty demands not falling into this confusion, which man falls into when he seeks self-realization. This pretense is illusory because human being and the essence of man are really distinct. In this sense the essence is called *detention.*

In sum, the third thesis states that if we do not abandon the mental limit, that is, if we do not clearly realize what presence, unicity, means, and if we do not go beyond it, then we cannot propose a transcendental anthropology. But, strictly speaking, neither can we formulate metaphysics axiomatically, nor develop the study of physical con-causality. For its part, the knowledge of God as principle of identity or origin is metaphysical. But there can also be a knowledge of God from anthropology.

This brief presentation brings together—in a nutshell—the overall thinking of the philosophy that I propose, the development of which all that I have been writing responds more or less to. Having said this, I will attempt to justify that the equivalence of *co-existing* and *"additionally"* (which is discovered following one of the ways of abandoning the limit) does not permit what is called "self-realization", if this term is not used in its current usage, which is rather vague.

Some indications about classical antecedents

I have presented in outline form the major themes that are made accessible by what I call the abandonment of the mental limit. Since they are notably different themes, it is important that the mental limit be abandoned in various ways or, as I often say, that it have various dimensions. It is a plural method with which the real distinction of Thomas Aquinas is recovered and applied to anthropology, something that is not normally done in spite of the fact that it is there, especially today, that the distinction of *essentia* and *esse* is most relevant. Hence, also the distinction between anthropology and metaphysics, without having to consider the former as a second philosophy. The being of man is superior to the being of the universe. Thus, it seems appropriate to apply the real distinction between *essentia* and *esse* in anthropology, since by this elevation of human being and of human essence one runs the risk of leaving its character as creature a bit in obscurity.

We were saying that extra-mental being or existence is accessed by abandoning the limit in the mode of adverting the strict meaning of the first principles. The knowledge of the first principles is the so-called *intellectus principiorum*, or habit of the first principles. Thus, up to this point, this abandonment of the limit seems to agree with (as a kind of development) the findings achieved by classical philosophy, although with a different terminology.

In turn, as I say, the extra-mental essence is explicitated. This is the abandonment of the limit in a second dimension. The extra-mental essence is the theme of the predicamental causes and the investigation of its correlations, etc. Causal physics was formulated by Aristotle. The corrections that I think are necessary center around the notion of *entelékheia*. And these have already been pointed out.

In a few of Thomas Aquinas's texts contained in the *Expositio in Boetii De Trinitate*, it is stated that the knowledge of principles can have two senses: the physical and the metaphysical. The physical sense is the knowledge of principles that are only principles. In Thomistic terminology, principles that, apart from being such, have no reason to be taken as *quidditative*. This is the concern of physics: the predicamental principles. And they are merely that: causes, as can clearly be gleaned from those texts. But then it can be asked why essence is mentioned, since it seems that essence has to do with the quidditative. However, as I see it, the physical essence, strictly speaking, is the consideration of the total con-causality, which I call quadruple. This follows from the abandonment of the limit and from the correction mentioned above. The consideration of the physical is exhausted if all the principles that are only principles are explicitated.

However, when it comes to metaphysical principles, Thomas Aquinas argues that their character as principle, which is with respect to what is grounded, must be distinguished from their proper nature, which is *quidditative* or essential. For this reason, the knowledge of these principles is double, since it is not the same to know that they are principles (which is arrived at from what is grounded) and to know their essence (which is not always achieved). Thomas Aquinas states that they are three: God, the soul, and (following the Aristotelian approach) the celestial bodies—the non-generable and incorruptible substances: the celestial spheres. Now, discarding the spheres (the stars are not as Aristotle thought them to be), what remains are the soul and God as principles with essence. In God the essence must be convertible with the originating identity, for which reason it is inaccessible. For its part, the soul is an anthropological topic. Can it be said with exactitude that the soul is principle and essence, or something more than principle? Metaphysically, yes (although it is not a first principle). But in anthropology it must be considered in some other way. Because, effectively, the soul is the immortal part of man's nature. But it is an essence that is really distinct from human *esse* inasmuch as it is habitually perfected. In turn, human *esse* is sufficiently distinct from the *esse* of the universe (which metaphysics studies) and cannot be said to be a first principle; neither can it be known with the habit of the first principles. For this reason, the principial character of the soul has to be dealt with carefully. With regard to the *esse hominis*, it thus no longer refers to a first principle. Although the immortality of the soul is accepted, it does not for this reason cease to be perfectible, and it must be kept in mind that without the knowledge of God, immortality is simple desolation. If the soul is understood as substance, it is reduced to ipseity and is separated from co-existence. If one accepts that it is *capax Dei*, then the act that saturates this capacity still remains to be discovered[5].

Furthermore, with the abandonment of the mental limit (which is unicity), one can *attain* human co-existence (the delay or detention in the essence, that is, essential coincidence with one's nature is also possible). In any case, it can be said that attaining human existence is, epistemologically, the habit of wisdom. The trans-objective knowledge of *esse hominis* is also a habitual knowledge (at least habitual); but it is a habit superior to the habit of the first principles.

The habit of wisdom is also known by classical philosophy. However, as I see it, it was studied very briefly or its moral connotations were simply highlighted. The very name "philosophy" marks out a certain distance from wisdom. On the other hand, this habit is not supernatural and the medieval theologians pay more attention to wisdom as a supernatural gift.

But this is not relevant here, since we are not presenting an anthropology of faith. The habit of wisdom manifests that the essence of man is not the *replica* of the human person and the problems that this entails.

---

5   It is impossible that the aforementioned act be an operation, since by saturating the capacity, it would have to be subsistent and the notion of subsistent operation cannot be admitted. In addition to this, if the *intellectus ut actus* is a personal transcendental, then no operation exhausts it, since the habits manifest the operations (it is also for this reason that the knowledge of God cannot be an operation since it makes no sense that it be manifested by another act). It is fitting to distinguish between the *intellectus ut actus*, the *intellectus ut habitus*, the intellective operations, and the *intellectus ut potentia*. On the other hand, the *voluntas ut natura* is a passive potency, according to Thomas Aquinas.

Self-realization and difference in anthropology

If the mental limit is the mental presence and if the mental presence is equivalent to the intellectual operations, then it makes sense to say that the human *esse* is *additionally* to the operations. Extra-mental being is adverted; in contrast, human being is attained—its superiority with respect to the mental presence is, so to speak, more intense. Attaining it from the limit is the character of *additionally*: knowing that which is expressed with this adverb.

What then is expressed by the adverb *additionally*? Well, with respect to the operations, that man is not exhausted in thinking (or in wanting). To say that man is a *res cogitans* is hasty. Being is not operating. It is said that man is *additionally* to operatively knowing, because human being is really distinguished from its essence, and operative thinking is of the order of the essentially manifest. Therefore, this distinction must also be manifest. And this means: human being is not destined to its essence, which, for this reason, is the non-available availing-of, the detention. The character of *additionally* is distinguished from detention—co-existence is not detained, nor arrives at a *terminus* (essential) or, as I often say, co-existence *lacks replica*. This lack is the essence of man.

Co-existence is not channeled, it is not attained, through the essential availing-of. The essence of man is the perfection of his nature, not of personal being, which is really distinct from it. And this is what the character of *additionally*, which is attained by the habit of wisdom, expresses. Habitual wisdom is nothing like the *noesis noeseos noesis*, but is rather the knowledge of the unsaturability of the *intellectus ut actus* by habits and operations. Although the perfectibility of man's nature is unrestricted, this is due to co-existence. The idea of infinitude is insufficient for co-existence (Duns Scotus falls short) because it does not accurately express that co-existence has no *terminus*. Neither does the immortality of the soul decide the question. It is the opposite: the immortality of the soul is due to co-existence, which either transcends infinitude or succumbs to the pure misfortune that monism is for co-existence. Person and absolute good; person and full truth; person and being, are expressions of this misfortune inasmuch as the good, the true, and being are metaphysical transcendentals, not anthropological ones, if behind them, the originating identity were not a person (*Deus Pater*), since co-existing would be left by itself[6].

I call the essence of man as perfection of his nature *detention*. Detention is availing-of; it is necessary to be detained in the availing-of so as not to confuse it with that which is available. The human person does not avail-of his essence, but rather in accordance with it. Detention indicates that essence is not the channel of co-existence, or rather, that co-existence cannot aspire to itself in terms of identity (identity is originating and not a result, and without the real distinction of essence and being there can be no creature), because this aspiration would isolate it or result in *solus ipse*. For its part, nature provides the dispositive modalities that are essentially perfected. These modalities have to be exercised.

Essence does not channel co-existence because it does not maintain the non-defuturization. And this is the detention. However, in another sense the essence is not detained—the dispositive modalities pass on to habit, and habit back to them, in such a way that the essence grows and the level of the operations rises. This back and forth of operations and habits is embellished by co-existence. Thus, the habit of the first principles is not followed by operations (the first principles are not within the reach of the dispositive modalities), and points to the superiority of freedom over the being of the universe. For its part, the habit of wisdom points to co-existing's

---

6   *Deus Pater, et Filius in sinu eius, et Spiritus Sanctus ab utroque.* The Holy Trinity is a revealed mystery. The desolation of monism for the person is uncovered by attaining the character of *additionally* through abandoning the mental limit. Except for desolation, the character of additionally entails the omnipotence and the mercy of God. Omnipotence and mercy are divine personal names *ad extra* (common) that are convertible with each other when the creature is person, and which express the *attraction* according to which co-existence is created (forgiving is also omnipotent mercy).

reference to the creator. It should be noted that these two habits are not symmetrical.

Beyond the symmetry with the being of universe, human freedom is transcendental. Freedom is an endowment upon which human essence depends. This dependence assures the availing-of, or rather, the essence on the level of habits. At the same time, human freedom is distinguished from the ground that is principle without freedom, not in the mode of a new principle, but rather as co-existence with respect to the principles—the relationship of co-existence to the being of the universe is not reciprocal, because the being of the universe does not co-exist. For this reason, the being of the universe in man is a habit. In other words, without prejudice to their independence (the being of the universe does not depend on man, because it is created), a new created dependence in accordance with the co-existence that is non-symmetric and lacking of replica is ascribed to. The expansion of the transcendental corrects modern philosophy. The symmetry with the ground is an unsuccessful expansion. Against this I propose: since the being of the universe does not co-exist, it is *habitually essentialized*.

Human co-existence is "essentializing" of the being of the universe, that is, it does not leave it to one side as a thing in itself. Since, however, man does not create the universe it should be said that he assimilates it habitually. It is not said that the essence of man is the essence of the universe, but rather that he endows it with that which the universe is incapable of. But the being of the universe is incapable, precisely, of "essentializing" itself, since it is really distinct from its essence.

By essentializing being, freedom is not confused nor identified with it, but rather co-exists with it, endowing it with that which it is incapable of. Here we have the exclusion of symmetry. The distinction of co-existence with respect to being is radical—it goes back to the being of the universe inasmuch as it essentializes it. Accordingly, human being can be described as that which perfects, or that which is ascribed to the universe according to the perfection that this is of itself incapable of[7].

One of the most notable features of modern philosophy is the interpretation of man according to his dynamisms. But a dynamic anthropology has the serious drawback of overburdening the natural dynamism of man with tasks that it cannot and has no reason to carry out, because the approach entails a double impoverishment: in the point of departure and in the result. It is not correct to attribute symbolic value to

---

7   Intersubjectivity in the human order, that is, the plurality of personal co-existences, still remains to be examined. It should be noted, first, that men possess the same nature or, better said, that the plurality of persons possesses a common nature. Without committing to the word, it is possible to speak of a human species, at least in the biological sense. Many aspects are registered on this level. For example, the duality of the sexes, and consequently, the institution of the family; history in its most elemental sense, as the non-contemporaneity of all human beings (birth and death); technology as condition for specific viability and the consequent division of labor, hostility and cooperation. These specific traits are complex. Since the nature of man is living, its community entails living together. And since persons are *called* to perfect their natures, living together is complex and problematic, because although their nature is common, their essence is not—each co-existent perfects nature to a greater or lesser degree, and also degrades it (some habits are *vices*). Nevertheless, in spite of the failures of living together (verifiable and abundant), the essences of co-existents entail *convocation*, not only because (verifiable) problems of living together *have to be* resolved, but because simply living together would not present problems if human beings had not availed-of in accordance with their essence (they are problems posed by a deficient "essentialization", and whose solutions lie in making up for this deficiency: it is inconsistent to have recourse for this reason to that which is available). On the other hand, the isolation of the person is tragic, as I have already stated, and, by lacking replica, recourse has to be made to the mediation of essences that I call convocation.

The convocation is society. According to Aristotle, men do not come together only to live together, but to live well; the good life is the virtuous life and dialogue. Human language is a habit and a mode of availing-of. Very important habits, such as truthfulness, mutual trust and friendship are linked to communication. In this way the *manifestive* character of the convocation of the co-exsistents' essences is highlighted. The manifestation arises from personal intimacy. I call this arising *inspiration*. Insofar as inspired, the manifestation is frequently *symbolic*. The symbols are expressions of the new. Strictly speaking, for each co-existent the other is not only the other, but also the *novum* (the plurality of the character of additionally entails—it is only possible this way—novelty, since it has to be compatible with de-futurization). Because they are expressive of the new, institutions and rites are supported by symbols and their crisis is due to the disappearance of this support.

what is dynamic, because in its point of departure it is not even formal.

Peculiar to modern philosophy is, for example, the notion of self-realization. If the being of man begins with a primary dynamism, then to speak of the reality of man is to speak of self-realization. But this is equivalent to entrusting human operating with a daunting task, and, moreover, one that is unnecessary and of little consequence. If, on the contrary, it is said that human being is additionally to the operation, to its natural endowment, or to its essential perfection, then there is no need to resort to the notion of self-realization. The real distinction *essentia-esse* implies that man does not essentially self-realize himself. For him to self-realize himself according to a dynamism it would be necessary that his essential endowment be a terminal achievement and identical with his being as a result, starting from an initial indetermination. But, I insist, this identification is incorrect with regard to God, that is, to the originating identity, and also in man, since the real distinction *essentia-esse* establishes the radical impossibility of self-realization, an ideal that nullifies the richness of the notion of creature; the creature is *extra nihilum*.

Although it is from something (in the sense that it requires actualizing a potentiality) self-realization places potency before act. For this reason, the approach is very mistaken. And in any case it is not properly anthropological, but rather an extrapolation of the metaphysical. The notion of *causa sui* is metaphysical. Therefore, the distinction of metaphysics and anthropology is highly fitting and appropriate. Otherwise, when one realizes that man is not only his operation, one can be tempted to entrust action with a task that reduces it to pure dynamism in search of an act, or whose act is the final result. This gives potency a character of being previous since it is the seeking for an act. The act is terminal, or as Hegel says, the absolute is the result. The notion of *causa sui* is untenable. It is nothing more than an erroneous way of referring to the absolute.

With the above, I attempt to highlight why the aforementioned adverbial denomination is appropriate for the being of man. If the character of additionally is attained by abandoning the limit, and if attaining the character of additionally is to know the *esse hominis*, then the *esse hominis* cannot be considered as *terminus* or as result or effect. For this reason the character of additionally is discovered in the abandonment of the operation, and not, in any way, according to the efficacy of the operation. If it were according to the efficacy of its acting, we would have a self-realization. Therefore, proposing that it is in the abandonment of the limit that one arrives at the major themes both in metaphysics as well as in anthropology (although according to distinct dimensions of the abandonment) is a way of controlling the approaches of modern philosophy, which is dominated by the notion of *causa sui* and by self-realization, or of the absolute as result.

Can it then be said that modern anthropology deals with human being? No. Therefore, it is not truly a transcendental anthropology. What does transcendental mean in modern philosophy? Well, what Kant says—the consideration of the logical as productive. If I consider the logical as non-productive, then logic is formal; if I consider the logical as condition of possibility, that is, as constitutive *a priori*, then I have transcendental logic. For Kant, transcendental logic is the consideration of an *a priori* that exercises an action over a product. The *Critique of Pure Reason* is constructed in accordance to this approach. In the end, Kant does not do anything more than physicalize reason or think it in terms of grounding. But this is not anthropology, but rather a symmetric interpretation of the ground.

In sum, self-realization is a grounding notion. The *causa sui* is also grounding. The discussion of all this belongs to metaphysics, but is foreign to anthropology, if it is the case that anthropology is sufficiently distinguished from metaphysics. Now, as I see it, this distinction is sufficiently established if the being and the essence of man are arrived at as themes that correspond to modes or dimensions of abandoning the mental limit that are distinct from those that allow for arriving at being and extra-mental essence.

Does the mental limit have to be abandoned in order to know being as principle and the predicamental principles? Yes. And precisely because human thinking is not causal. Therefore, there will be dimensions of the abandonment of the limit that consist in the advertence [*advertencia*] of the distinction between the limit and the causal, or grounding. The mental limit is the immanent operation. And immanent operations do not act as principles since they possess ideologically. This way of possessing has absolutely nothing to do with production or with the notion of cause. The metaphysical thematic requires an adequate distinction of the principles with respect to the immanent operation. And this adequate distinction implies that the operation is detected as limit.

Having gone over the four dimensions of the limit, this thesis can be established: the knowledge of the ground is the knowledge of what is distinct from the limit, because the mental limit is not ground. The mental limit is the operation, and the operation is the knowledge of the object; but the object is intentional, and is not groundingly real. In no way is the intentional real. And even less so is it a principle. Here, the abandonment of the limit is therefore the realization that if principles exist, those principles are extra-mental. Therefore, it can also be said that the theme of metaphysics (and of physics) is extra-mental being and extra-mental essence.

At the same time, in order to know that which is human, the limit must be abandoned in such as way that it does not bring us to the extra-mental, but rather, so to speak, that it keeps us in what is human. How is one kept in what is human when it comes to being? By stating that human being is not a principle or a ground (of the operation), because that belongs to the extra-mental, and human being is not extra-mental, but rather additionally to the mental. This additionally is not a first

54

principle and, inversely, neither can it be said that the first principle is additionally.

Metaphysics deals with existence (with the being that exists); anthropology, as expansion of the transcendental, deals with being as co-existing or co-existence. One arrives at human co-existence insofar as additionally to the mental, not insofar as extra-mental. And being additionally is convertible with co-existence. One catches a glimpse of the coherence between the distinction of anthropology and metaphysics; and the abandonment of the mental limit as method for accessing the major themes of being and of essence[8].

If the operation of thinking and the intentional object are not transcended, it is not possible to arrive at the real as real. Intentional knowledge is a valid way of knowing; but it is aspectual. Abandoning the mental limit is not an appeal to the will or to feelings in order then to make a metaphysics or an anthropology of a voluntaristic or sentimental type. Nothing like that. From Aristotle, I take radical intellectualism, but it does not seem to me that human knowing is only operative, or that the operation is the highest mode of knowing. It has frequently been noted that objective knowledge is limited.

A brief reference to ethics. It is evident that traditional morality is more correct than modern moralities. But this is because, having realized the importance of freedom in man, it is concluded that I construct the morality that I want. Because only from freedom can I construct a morality, and if I construct from freedom, then I do not construct it from nature. Ultimately, one ends up saying that man has no nature. However, a morality that has nothing to do with nature (a situational or consequentialist morality; either absolute or autonomous; or an ineffective morality, pure sentimental intuition of values, etc.) is very weak in practice. Now, if the modern approaches do not lead to a well-justified morality,

---

8 It is clear that Thomas Aquinas frequently makes use of a causal approach, even when dealing with man. But Thomas Aquinas does not develop anthropology very much; rather, he moves more on the metaphysical plane. I have already said: this is not incorrect, although I propose to go further.

this is because freedom exercises strong pressure over nature, because it is interpreted as force, as arbitrary spontaneity. This is physicalism or, in any case, pseudo-metaphysics. For this reason, if anthropology is adequately distinguished from metaphysics, if (so to speak) it leaves it at peace and does not harass it, then freedom is not confused with the ground and the difficulties of modern ethics are avoided. The essence of man does not leave out nature. If one accepts human essence, then with all the more reason one must say that there is a human nature, because the essence is the culminating consideration of nature.

I insist. Insofar as we burden metaphysics with anthropological questions, the result is bad metaphysics and bad anthropology (for example with the interpretation of freedom as spontaneity or as force). It can also happen that one realizes that freedom is not a force. And then one concludes that freedom does not exist. If freedom lacks force, then, since it is forces that are sought for, freedom is liquidated. Or the opposite can happen—since freedom exists, I have to interpret it as absolute force, as a radically primary force. Therefore, man has to freely make himself. In both cases a type of confusion is produced. In one case, freedom is denied, because of its not being the ground; and in the other, freedom is undermined by interpreting it as ground.

For this reason, although what is said here is not in Aristotle, it seems to me that it captures the spirit of Aristotelian philosophy. On the other hand, if one considers the distinctions that Thomas Aquinas formulates, and compares them with that of modern authors, then it can be noted that the latter are obsessed with identity (which for them is formal; it is a mere logical identity); the differences become few or they are not sufficiently precise. Aristotle's genius is a discerning genius, because he is a great observer. Here is the key for developing Aristotle and, nevertheless, of preserving the spirit of Aristotle, or rather, of not ceasing to be Aristotelian when dealing with themes that he did not deal with.

Does Aristotle sufficiently distinguish man from what is not man? The expansion of the transcendental implies the difference between existence and co-existence. Aristotle understood this difference as specific difference: man is the only rational animal and the only rational being that is animal. There is evidently a difference here. But, is the specific difference enough? I believe that is it not, because the person is not definable, but rather is transcendental. Therefore, the person should be a distinction in the order of the transcendentals. Or, in other words, the expansion of the transcendental has to be a discernment of transcendentals. The expansion of the transcendental distinguishes that which is transcendental with respect to the physical from the personal transcendental. It discovers transcendentals that are not trans-physical or trans-definitional (in the general sense that definition has for Aristotle), but rather are trans-operative. And this is what *additionally* means—it is the way to access human *esse*.

Other indications regarding the character of *additionally*

I have tried to distinguish the advertence of extra-mental being from the attainment of human being. In order to advert extra-mental being, the habit of the first principles is needed. Objective knowledge is not enough. In order to know the causes, they have to be explicitated precisely inasmuch as they are contradistinct from the mental operations, because the mental operation is not a cause, nor the ground, nor anything like it. Now, abandoning the mental operations in no way means calling into question its value. The abandonment of the limit is not a critique of objective knowledge. Critical philosophy is Kantian; uncovering differences is not criticizing or discrediting. Discerning does not diminish the value of the object. Operative knowledge is valid. And also what is distinct from it. A philosophy of difference is, if you will, a philosophy of *also*. In it the character of *additionally* has to appear in order to play a major role.

Now, can it be said that the extra-mental is *additionally* to the operation? No. It has to simply be said that it is extra-mental, that it is not known by the operation, or that this is insufficient for it. It is known by a habit, but it is not an *additionally* that is intrinsically *additionally*, that is, a character of the theme itself. In contrast, when it comes to human existence, since strictly speaking it has to do with the order of the human, that is, since it cannot regard anything external to man, with respect to which the extra-mental is external, but rather (so to speak) it is an insisting on the human, beyond the operation, then it can be said that human existence is precisely *additionally* to the operation. And precisely because it is so, it is intrinsically described as co-existence[9].

What is under discussion in modern philosophy is the theme of freedom, the theme of the subject. Anthropocentrism, etc. is spoken of. But, isn't an inquiry within this order needed, precisely in order to point out the inadequacy of the modern treatment of these topics? And it is not for this reason that it must to be interpreted *in peius*. Rather, it is a question of continuing what the moderns glimpsed but were not capable of developing because of their having discarded the habits of classical inspiration, and of expanding the classical thematic. Therefore, it is not a question of originality. What there is, is an attempt to once again take up themes that were left hanging, that are more or less declared, but seen or outlined in a confused way. And since doing philosophy is doing philosophy today (philosophy is not something of the past), it turns out that this focus is appropriate. Appropriate is

---

9 All this is difficult to say. They are approaches that come to mind or are discovered before saying them; for this reason they become rather tangled when they are expressed. The language has to be forced, has to be struggled with. I am trying to communicate a proposal to you. That it has occurred to me does not mean any originality whatsoever. Originality is not a philosophical value. I simply present it, seeking to come to terms with modern philosophy and to continue classical philosophy.

what is fitting now; and now it is fitting to face modern philosophy and, on the other hand, to develop and complete the philosophy of classical inspiration. But, correctly understood—classical inspiration is not something of the past, but rather an inspiration that has to be valid today. In any case, since it is clear that the anthropological questions have been one of the major central themes of modern philosophers' attention, although dealt with in a rather incorrect way, as I will later try to justify even more, it is clear that this is what has to be done.

If I am not limited to thinking, precisely because thinking is the limit, then I am *additionally*. *Additionally* to what? First of all, *additionally* to thinking. For this reason, *cogito ergo sum* is not enough. Better: *cogito* and *additionally sum*; *cogito ergo sum* subordinates the *sum* to the *cogito* and concludes that I am a *res cogitans*. But, no—instead, one must say *cogito* and *additionally sum*. It is not the same. Therefore, it is not that *sum* is added to *cogito* or latches onto *cogitare*. No. *Additionally* does not mean adding, nor is it something added, but rather it signifies *being beyond* and it is in this beyond where additionally *is*. Or rather, this beyond is maintained as beyond in terms of *additionally*. The beyond is *additionally*, not a mere addition to thinking, nor a ratification of thinking (*cogito ergo sum*). And, therefore, *additionally* is a designation of act of being.

In any case, there is no reason for saying that this designation of the act of being corresponds to the first principles. Human being is *additionally*. And that it is additionally means that it is not exhausted in an actual consideration; that it is act, but is not actuality. In contrast, the act of thinking is act, but actual act. If I am *additionally*, I am not a mere actual act, because according to actuality I would be consumed, I would not be additionally. The operation of knowing is enough. Each operation of knowing is commensurate with its object, and therefore is enough. But being enough is limit. And it certainly is with respect to my being, because my being is a pure overflowing. And this means act; but not actual act, but rather *additionally* act.

"You said enough and then perished" [*dixisti statis ibi peristi*] (St. Augustine [Sermon 169, 15]). Now, thinking is enough; nevertheless, thinking does not perish. Because the act of thinking is actual; it is presence (mental presence), precisely because it is enough for the object, and the object is enough for the act of thinking. This is what I call the *axiom of commensuration.* The act of knowing is commensurate with the object; the object is commensurate with the operation. This being enough is the mental limit. In contrast, the being of man is not commensurate with the object. And precisely because it is not commensurate, it is co-existence, *additionally. Additionally* is equivalent, in transcendental equivalence, with co-existing.

Coexisting is *additionally.* One co-exists only if one is additionally. Or, put in another way, one co exists if one is worthy. And this being worthy is something more than the value of which Max Scheler speaks, or value in Nietzsche's sense. Human being is a being that is worthy. And precisely for this reason, he is moral in his essence. Morality is a question of capacity, because not every essence is capable of fulfilling a moral norm.

Sometimes it is said that the moral is a constraint. Absolutely false. This is a perspective that depends on the notion of self-realization. But *additionally* is beyond self-realization. Being *additionally* is an overflowing; and by being an overflowing it gives of itself. This is much more than Nietzsche's will to power.

If man is considered apart from the moral, then he is considered as incapable of the moral. It is not that it is a legitimate aspiration, but rather that it is inalienable, because if man renounces it, he lowers himself. If I do not live according to a morality, this means that I would not be capable of it. Being moral is always *being capable-of.* Morals have to do with human dignity and human dignity is the person. In turn, a morality without virtues is partial. What is virtue? Growth in the order of capacity. Thus, if one gives up morality, one ceases to grow. Growing is much more than self-realization, because to realize oneself is to place the absolute in the *terminus.* In contrast, growing is precisely being beyond the *terminus.* Is the absolute the result? With this, one is thinking the absolute apart from growth, because the absolute as result is nothing more than a balance, and is, moreover, insuperable—there is nothing more. But growth is precisely being more capable.

However, all this—being more capable, virtue—belongs to the order of the human essence. But this is so in the order of essence because in the order of co-existence and of *esse* the character of *additionally* is attained. For this reason, I say that human essence can be described as *availing-of.* The designation of human essence as availing-of inevitably points to freedom as transcendental, to a being that is freedom. Because freedom is convertible with *additionally.* If I am additionally, I am free. Free, which does not mean arbitrary. No. Freedom is the richness of my being. This richness of my being in the essence is the growth of my capacity; for example, my moral capacity. Am I capable of morality? Yes. Now, does morality have a terminative character for me? No. Why? Because insofar as I am moral, I grow in virtue. Therefore, I do not end. For this reason, it is not valid to hold that the absolute is the result.

With this we have made a little bit of progress on a difficult issue. Because suddenly taking up the character of additionally can give rise to an inexpressible philosophy, or one so far removed from normal formation that it can appear as an occurrence of some pseudo-genius. "Character of additionally?" "One more occurrence in these extravagant times!"; "See—each one with their particular knowledge!" To understand it, one must first be acquainted with some kind of great philosophy. For example, it is necessary to know what a mental operation is, something that not everyone knows.

I think and additionally I am, or I am additionally to thinking. Because additionally is, first of all, additionally to mental operation. If I think, the being that corresponds to me is additionally—my being is additionally. With this, Descartes is left behind. *Cogito* and additionally *sum.* And furthermore in such a way that it is additionally with respect to *cogito.* And it is additionally with respect to the *cogito* in such a way that this additionally is maintained as additionally. That is, it is act—something that the *sum* is not in Descartes. The Cartesian *sum* is nothing more than an existential quantifier.

And this is, on the other hand, what Kant reproaches him for when he points out that the *cogito sum* is a paralogism. Descartes deals with empirical reality. And for this reason the middle term is not universal. But the *sum* of the "I think in general" (*Ich denke Überhaupt*, that is, the transcendental conscience) cannot be empirical, because it is in the logical-transcendental order. Thus, the Cartesian *sum* is empirical. The Kantian criticism is valid, in spite of fact that the *cogito ergo sum* is not a syllogism and Kant treats it as if it were. It is not that there is a paralogism, because Descartes is not making a syllogism. He thinks that *cogito-sum* is an intuition. And therefore one must say that the way that Descartes arrives at the *sum* from the *cogito* does not allow finding the human *sum*. In order to avoid understanding the *sum* as an existential quantifier (neither is it correct to take it as a universal), one must attain it—it is additionally-act, an act whose intrinsic character is *additionally*, an inexhaustible act as *actus essendi*.

The principle of immanence and the principle of transcendence are often spoken of. And this is not correct, because the principle of immanence, strictly speaking, is not such a principle. Rather it is this: immanent operation; and act of being *additionally*. It is a transcending with the character of additionally. In contrast, going from immanence to metaphysics, that is, to the metaphysical or principial act of being, is not a transcending with the character of *additionally*.

The character of additionally makes it possible to understand that human being is inexhaustible as act. Therefore, that it is not consumed in a result, but rather redounds in the essence as perfection of nature even though this is not its replica. In no way is it *causa sui*. With the notion of *causa sui* the only thing that is achieved is to satisfy a necessity, to establish a balance—it is *causa sui*, and that's it.

But it cannot be said of human being that it "already is", because the *already* is a characteristic of the object.

And what does this inexhaustibility express? First of all it can be said: freedom. Because being additionally is not depending on necessity, not being tied down (like the being of Parmenides). And this is transcendental freedom, not freedom of choice, because one chooses in function of a motive or in order to possess something one does not have, etc. Choice belongs to the order of man's practical projects. Because man, from the point of view of his nature, needs. But considering his being, that is, his personal character, being free means maintaining oneself in *additionally*, that is, in being that co-exists. As I said, *additionally* is not the *mónon*. The *mónon* has already reached its fulfillment; and, thus, the only thing that can be done is to deviate downward, something like a decompression. Or rather to give rise to an infinite series of attributes, like Leibniz's monad.

Additionally is more than emerging, because emerging refers to what emerges, and emerging has something terminative to it. This is the old notion of the pre-Socratic *physis*, the first philosophical formulation. *Physis* is the verbal genesis of a noun. As such, on the one hand it is a verb, an emerging; but a verb that seeks consistency, an actual fixity, and is consumed according to this actual fixity. And it is thereby a verb and a noun. But the character of additionally is neither a verb nor a noun. For this reason, I turn to an adverbial expression.

What has been abandoned by *additionally* is the supposition. Because presence means supposition of the object. Strictly speaking the object is what is supposed. The distinction between suppositions, for example, Ockham's and even the earlier ones (the more or less Platonic ones discovered by earlier medieval thinkers), are logical senses of the supposition, derived senses.

Now, if the mental limit, the supposition, is abandoned then *additionally* is attained. If it is supposited, then it can no longer be said to be *additionally*, because suppositing is fixing. But *additionally* is a completely actuous act, not actual; and, therefore, free. Here the act is maintained; and by being in the maintaining, it is inexhaustible.

Actus essendi-essentia. This *actus essendi* is not static, but rather it is precisely actuosity—not actuating act, but rather actuosity. A metaphor for actuosity is the flame that is not consumed; like the burning bush of *Exodus*: a fire that neither is consumed nor consumes. Ultimately, it is the Holy Spirit. To burn like this, this is spirit. *Additionally* is the co-existing, created human spiritual being.

These repeated attempts at providing indications regarding the character of additionally are due to its enormous difficulty; it is difficult because it is not an object.

Fabro speaks of intensive act. But intensity is like a kind of concentration or densification. *Additionally* is not a greater intensity of act. Intensity is along the lines of the search for unity, for *mónon*. But an act that focuses on itself remains there. And the being of man does not remain—it is co-existing, in such a way that it is in the co-existing. Intensity is an attempt from within the metaphysical order. To think of the intensity would be to think of the unity of the act of being.

[In contrast, *additionally* is not the unity of the act of being, but rather it is more than the unity of the act of being—it is inexhaustible emerging; it is freedom. Freedom is also more than unity, more than *unum*.]*

---

* This last paragraph was not published in the Spanish editions. We have, however, decided to include it here from an earlier digital draft.

Books by Leonardo Polo

1. *Evidencia y realidad en Descartes.* (Madrid: Rialp, 1963; Pamplona: Eunsa, 1996 (2nd ed.); 2007 (3rd ed.))

2. *El acceso al ser.* (Pamplona: Universidad de Navarra, 1964; Pamplona: Eunsa 2004 (2nd ed.))

3. *El ser I: la existencia extramental.* (Pamplona: Universidad de Navarra, 1966; Pamplona: Eunsa 1997 (2nd ed.))

4. *Curso de teoría del conocimiento, v. I.* (Pamplona: Eunsa, 1984; 1987 (2nd ed.); 2006 (3rd ed.))

5. *Curso de teoría del conocimiento, v. II.* (Pamplona: Eunsa, 1985; 1988 (2nd ed.); 1998 (3rd ed.); 2006 (4th ed.))

6. *Hegel y el posthegelianismo.* (Piura (Peru): Universidad de Piura, 1985; Spanish reprints: Pamplona: Eunsa 1999 (2nd ed.); 2006 (3rd ed.))

7. *Curso de teoría del conocimiento, v. III.* (Pamplona: Eunsa, 1988; 1999 (2nd ed.); 2006 (3rd ed.))

8. *¿Quién es el hombre? Un espíritu en el tiempo.* (Madrid: Rialp, 1991; 1993 (2nd ed.); 1998 (3rd ed.); 2001 (4th ed.); 2003 (5th ed.); 2007 (6th ed.); South American Edition: Piura (Peru): Universidad de Piura, 1993)

   –Italian translation: *Chi é l'uomo: uno spirito nel tempo.* Trans. Patrizia Bonagura. Milan (Italy): Vita e pensiero, 1992

10. *El conocimiento habitual de los primeros principios.* (Pamplona: Universidad de Navarra, 1993; Included in Nominalismo, idealismo y realismo (1997), parte III)

11. *Etica: hacia una versión moderna de los temas clásicos.* (Mexico City (Mexico): Universidad Panamericana/Publicaciones

Cruz O., 1993; Spanish reprints: Madrid: Unión editorial (AEDOS), 1996; 1997 (2nd ed.))

–English translation: *Ethics. A modern version of its classic themes.* Paul Arvisu Dumol. (Manila (Philippines): Sinag-Tala Publishers 2008)

–Partial Portuguese translation online: *A ética e a teoria da evoluçao.*

12. *Presente y futuro del hombre.* (Madrid: Rialp, 1993; 2012 (2nd ed.))

13. *Curso de teoría del conocimiento, v. IV / 1st Part.* (Pamplona: Eunsa, 1994)

    –2nd edition together with 2nd Part: Pamplona: Eunsa 2004

14. *Introducción a la filosofía.* (Eunsa, 1995; 1999 (2nd ed.); 2002 (3rd ed.))

15. *Curso de teoría del conocimiento, v. IV / 2nd Part.* (Pamplona: Eunsa, 1996)

    –2nd edition together with 1st Part: Pamplona: Eunsa 2004

16. *La persona humana y su crecimiento.* (Pamplona: Eunsa, 1996; 1999 (2nd ed.))

17. *Sobre la existencia cristiana.* (Pamplona: Eunsa, 1996)

    –2nd edition titled *La originalidad de la concepción cristiana de la existencia.* (Pamplona: Eunsa, 2010 (2nd ed.))

18. *Antropología de la acción directiva.* (with C. Llano) (Madrid: Unión editorial (AEDOS), 1997)

19. *Nominalismo, idealismo y realismo.* (Pamplona: Eunsa, 1997; 2001 (2nd ed.))

20. *La voluntad y sus actos (I).* (Pamplona: Universidad de Navarra, 1998)

21. *La voluntad y sus actos (II).* (Pamplona: Universidad de Navarra, 1998)

22. *Antropología trascendental I: la persona humana.* (Pamplona: Eunsa, 1999; 2003 (2nd ed.); 2010 (3rd ed.))

23. *Antropología trascendental II: la esencia de la persona humana.* (Pamplona: Eunsa, 2003; 2010 (2nd ed.))

24. *El conocimiento racional de la realidad.* (Pamplona: Universidad de Navarra 2004)

25. *El yo.* (Pamplona: Universidad de Navarra, 2004)

26. *El orden predicamental.* (Universidad de Navarra, 2005)

27. *La crítica kantiana del conocimiento.* (Pamplona: Universidad de Navarra, 2005)

    –Portuguese translation (Medeiros-Do Amaral; IBFC Raimundo Lulio): *A crítica kantiana do conhecimento.* Colección Grandes obras do pensamento universal, n° 85. Sao Paulo (Brasil): Escala, 2007

28. *La libertad trascendental.* (Pamplona: Universidad de Navarra, 2005)

29. *Lo radical y la libertad.* (Pamplona: Universidad de Navarra, 2005)

30. *Nietzsche como pensador de dualidades.* (Pamplona: Eunsa, 2005)

31. *La esencia humana.* (Pamplona: Universidad de Navarra, 2006)

32. *Ayudar a crecer. Cuestiones filosóficas de la educación.* (Pamplona: Eunsa, 2006; 1st reprinting, 2007)

33. *El logos predicamental.* (Pamplona: Universidad de Navarra, 2006)

34. *Las organizaciones primarias y las empresas.* (Pamplona: Universidad de Navarra, 2007)

35. *Persona y libertad.* (Pamplona: Eunsa, 2007)

36. *El conocimiento del universo físico.* (Pamplona: Eunsa, 2008)

37. *El hombre en la historia.* (Pamplona: Universidad de Navarra, 2008)

38. *Lecciones de psicología clásica.* (Pamplona: Eunsa, 2009)

39. *Curso de psicología general.* (Pamplona: Eunsa, 2009, 2010 (2nd ed.))

40. *Introducción a Hegel.* (Pamplona: Universidad de Navarra, 2010)

41. *La esencia del hombre.* (Pamplona: Eunsa, 2011)

42. *Filosofía y economía.* (Pamplona: Eunsa, 2012)

43. *Estudios de filosofía moderna y contemporánea.* (Pamplona: Eunsa, 2012)

44. *Lecciones de ética.* (Pamplona: Eunsa, Pamplona, 2013)

45. *Epistemología, creación y divinidad.* (Pamplona: Eunsa, Pamplona, 2014)

61834161R00059

Made in the USA
Lexington, KY
22 March 2017